Girlz Want to Know

01 02 03 04 05 06/❖ DC/ 10 9 8 7 6 5 4 3 2 1

Young Women of Faith

Girlz Want to Know

Answers to Real–Life Questions

Written by Susie Shellenberger

Zonder**kidz**
The Children's Group of ZondervanPublishingHouse

❀ ❀ ❀

Dedicated to Jennifer, Mallory,

and Stephanie Bergland.

I'm privileged to have you in my life.

Contents

Q. My dad was recently diagnosed with cancer. Sometimes he's in a lot of pain. He works a lot, and when he is home, it seems as if he and my mom are always going on walks together. I need him, too!

A. I'm so sorry your dad is fighting the tough battle of cancer. He's probably frightened and wondering how much time he has left. That must be scary for you as well.

If his days are numbered, he may be spending more time with your mom to ensure that everything's taken care of. For example, they may be talking about insurance, savings, the money for your future college years, etc. He probably wants to make sure your family will be well provided for after he's gone. And they may feel it's inappropriate, or too disturbing, to include you and your brothers or sisters in these conversations.

And though it seems he's spending extra time with your mom, he may not even realize that the two of you haven't had much time together recently. Why not bake his favorite dessert? Or rent one of his all-time fave videos, make some popcorn, and curl up on the couch with him.

Ask if the two of you can have a dad-daughter date, and tell him how much you love him. Meanwhile, since you know he's in physical pain, pray for him and be patient with him.

Q. Every person in my family is or was addicted to something. Can that be passed down in the genes?

A. Yes and no. Let's take it slow and simple, okay? There *is* such a thing as having a predisposition to addiction. That means you may have tendencies toward addiction. But if you know that, you can certainly learn to make wise choices to stay away from addictive things.

We all have free choice. Your family may be predisposed toward addictive behavior, but that doesn't mean there's no hope. You don't *have* to become addicted.

God doesn't want anyone to be addicted to anything. Have you asked him for help? Why don't we pray about it right now, okay?

Dear Jesus:

It makes me sad that everyone in my family is, or has been, addicted to something. I don't want to become an addict. Will you take control of my life? I want to give myself totally to you, Jesus. Please help me to stay completely away from anything that could become addictive such as cigarettes, alcohol, drugs, pornography, and (fill in the blank with anything else you can think of).

Guide me, Father. Teach me how to make wise choices. I love you, and I'll trust you with my life. Amen.

Q. My seven-year-old brother loves to get me in trouble. I don't know what to do to make him stop. I've told my parents, but they don't do anything about it. How can I make him stop?

A. This may not be the answer you're wanting, but here goes. You probably *can't* make him stop. None of us can control other people's behavior. But here's the good news: This is an important lesson for you to learn. Why? Because we go through our entire lives having to deal with people who don't behave right, and the sooner we learn to handle it, the better.

Even though he's saying stuff to get you in trouble, promise God that you'll always be honest. People often get accused of something that wasn't their fault, and there's no defense. It's not fair, but it happens. God knows your heart, and he can help you endure the consequences of your brother's behavior—even though you're not to blame. Jesus was crucified on a cross, and he was completely innocent. He has the power to help you in similar situations.

There will probably be others in your life who will blame you for something you didn't do, or tell lies about you. Keep being honest. Eventually, those around you will see you as a young lady of integrity and great character. And the dishonesty in others will be seen as well.

One more thing: Even though you may get in trouble when you don't deserve it . . . you can still feel really good about yourself by knowing you're an honest girl. Always tell the truth.

Q. My mom and I just don't communicate well. I've tried and tried to talk with her, but she just won't listen. It seems I have to yell just to get her to pay attention to me. Then she says I'm out of control and won't answer any of my questions. But she doesn't listen to me when I'm calm, either. What should I do?

A. It's frustrating when we're trying to communicate with someone and we feel we're being ignored, isn't it? Timing is everything. In other words, *when* are you trying to talk with your mom? Is it as soon as she comes through the door from a long day at work and is juggling four bags of groceries? Bad timing.

Is it when she's hurriedly trying to get dinner on the table before your dad gets home? Bad timing.

I suggest writing her a note and telling her some really important stuff—like how much you love her, and that you appreciate all she does for your family. Then ask her if there's a specific time, every day or even twice a week, that just the two of you can spend together.

It might be that she can sit on the edge of your bed for 15 minutes before you nod off. Or it could be that you can help her with the laundry every Thursday evening and talk then. In the note, make it clear to her that you want time together to talk. Then let her tell you when the best time will be. Chances are you'll get her undivided attention . . . without yelling.

Q. Um ... okay, this is really hard, but I need to say it. Today something really scary happened. My dad hit my mom. He didnt hit her hard, but he hit her. This is totally unlike him! If you knew him, you'd be shocked.

I talked to him about it, but he wouldn't say much ... except that he wouldn't do it again. I don't know if I can believe that. I'm really scared! What if he does it again?

A. I'm so sorry this happened! And I can understand why you're so scared. It's frightening to see our family members experience and be a part of something so destructive.

Try to realize that your dad is hurting right now. That's still not an excuse for hitting your mom (there's *never* an excuse for hitting someone you love). If it happens again, you need to tell someone. It will be hard, but you'll need to tell your pastor, your youth leader, a teacher, or a school counselor. They will inform the authorities; and, yes, the authorities need to be involved.

Maybe this was just a one-time thing. Maybe not. Please talk with your mom. Tell her you know what happened. Tell her how scared you are. Listen to what she has to say. And let her know if it happens again, you *will* tell. Then ask if the two of you can pray together.

Q. My parents are always telling me what to do, and I'm sick of it! Help!

A. The older we get, the less we feel we need instruction from our parents. But since they have a few years on you, they can see what you can't, and they want to warn, guide, and help you during these special years of your life.

God has created a unique power structure that involves both you and your folks. Think of it as a pyramid. God is on top—He's the most important. Right under him is your parents. And you're underneath your parents. He's in authority over your folks, and they're in authority over you.

When all three levels of the pyramid are in sync with each other, things run as God intended. But when one level rebels against the other, trouble brews. Even if your parents are not Christians, God wants you to do your part. You honor God by obeying your mom and dad.

God placed your parents in your life for a special reason: He loves you so much, he didn't want you to have to try and figure out life on your own. When you think of it this way, it's exciting to realize that you can actually get a lot *from* your parents—wisdom, love, guidance.

Pray for your parents. They're not perfect; not one of us is. There will come a day when your parents will quit telling you what to do, but it's going to be a few years. Meanwhile, prove your maturity to them by simply obeying.

Q. *What can I get my mom for Mother's Day?*

A. How about something from your heart? Moms *love* it when we make them things. I remember making my mom several items when I was a little girl, and guess what! She still has them! Moms treasure everything their daughters make, because those are the things that can't be bought—they come straight from the heart.

I'll list a few ideas, and you fill in the list with some of your own, okay?

- Coupon book. *Create several different coupons for a variety of special services such as "good for one housecleaning any time you ask," "good for one back rub," "good for a hug" (make several of these!), "good for a free macaroni and cheese dinner made by me."*
- Bible bookmark. *Make a special bookmark that your mom can use for her Bible or another favorite book.*
- Photo memories. *Find (or have a friend take) a special photograph of you and your mom. Make your own frame, and write your favorite Scripture on the back.*

Q. My mom is driving me crazy! After I've gone to school, she goes into my room and throws everything I haven't put away into my closet. I've asked her not to do this, but she does it anyway. Last week I left some things around my stereo, and she tossed it all into my closet.

My other friends get to have messy rooms, why can't I? It makes me want to go into her room and throw all her stuff in the closet. Ugh!

A. Let's imagine that you've built a really cool tree house—nothing fancy—just a small but fun place you and a couple of girlfriends can climb to at the top of the old oak tree in your backyard. You love the rustic and open feel of it! And when the wind is up, you can feel the breeze sail right through your hair. It's a great place for you to unwind and think. One day Ashley brings a piece of brand-new carpet her dad let her have from re-carpeting their living room. It's beautiful, and she wants to donate it to the tree house. But you don't *want* carpet in the tree house. You like the rough look. Since you own the tree house, it's only fair that you get to decide how it looks.

Since your mom (and dad) is paying the bills for your home, it makes sense that she has the say about how she wants it to look. And while it doesn't bother *you* to have things out of place, it obviously gets on Mom's nerves.

Ask her for a time when the two of you can talk uninterrupted, and explain that while you understand her desire to have everything in its place, you're feeling a need for a little flexibility. Ask if there are specific areas in your room over which you can have absolute control. For instance, she may not want things lying around your stereo, but is it okay to keep a little pile on your desk or under your bed?

Maybe the two of you can compromise. But if she still says no, you've gotta respect her decision. Someday you'll have your own house, and *you'll* get to decide how it looks!

Q. My mom and I argue a lot, and when my dad joins in I feel ganged-up on. We're all Christians, but Mom and I are strong-willed. We both tend to think we're right. I need to talk with someone. My sister is married and has her own life, and I don't want to talk with my friends about this. What can I do?

A. I admire you for wanting to talk with someone who can help you make the situation better. But first let's talk about what's happening before we decide what you can do about it and whom you can talk with, okay?

There might be a *reason* your dad is joining in on the arguments you're having with your mom. Since you've already stated that you're strong-willed, I'm guessing that no matter what your mom says, you probably argue with her. Maybe it *takes* both your mom *and* your dad to make sure you get what they're trying to say.

Think about it: If you quit arguing with your mom, and simply accepted what she said, your dad wouldn't have a reason to join in, would he?

Try this: The next time you feel an argument beginning to brew between you and your mom, silently ask

God to help you *not* to fight. Did you know you can disagree without arguing? Try something like this, "Mom, I don't see it that way, but you're in charge. Okay." Or, "I don't agree, but I respect you and I'm going to obey. But can we pray about it together?"

These kinds of approaches to your mom will show her that you're not just trying to get your way all the time, but that you're willing to submit to her authority even when you don't agree. In time, the two of you will probably be able to discuss the reasons *behind* her answers. But first, you need to show her you're able to obey without putting up a fight.

Q. I love computers, but my mom won't let me go into chat rooms. What gives?

A. What gives is that you have a very wise mom. She knows a few things about chat rooms that you don't. They can be extremely dangerous. Even though someone may *say* she's fifteen years old and wants to make a new friend, "she" can actually be a thirty-five-year-old male who's trying to find an innocent and trusting girl he can take advantage of.

Never, never, never, *ever* give out your name, phone number, or address over the Internet. I know of a case in Colorado where a teen girl struck up a friendship with a teen guy. After a few weeks of chatting online, they decided to meet at a motel, and the "teen guy" ended up being a middle-aged man who wanted to become sexually involved with a teenager.

My advice? Listen to your mom and stay outta the chat rooms!

Q. *My sister and I fight a lot. Even though she's three years younger than I am, we're the same size. She's kind of a tomboy and tries to wrestle me. When I do something to defend myself, she ends up crying and tells my mom. I always get in trouble. What should I do?*

A. Ask your parents if you can talk with them privately—just the three of you. Explain your side to them and ask if they'll consider all of you getting together to create a nonnegotiable policy for all family relationships. Everyone gets to have his or her say, but your parents will decide which "rules" stay on the final cut of the family policy.

Here are a few examples that I'd list on the policy:

- *No one is allowed to harass the other verbally or physically.*
- *No one is allowed to lie.*
- *No one is allowed to take something that doesn't belong to him without asking.*

You've probably heard of contemporary Christian artist Rebecca St. James. I traveled with her and her family for two Christmas seasons as she did her Christmas concert tour, and I was really impressed how smoothly things went inside this large family (seven kids)! Their policy is "No secrets."

Try it.

Q. We have youth group on Wednesday nights at our church. It's a great time of fun and hanging out with friends. But it's also a time where we can pray together and learn more about God.

The problem is, whenever I get in trouble at home, my mom grounds me from going to youth group. Everyone in my family is a Christian, so it's not like she doesn't understand what youth group is all about.

I hate missing it! And I don't mean to get in trouble; sometimes it just happens. What can I do?

A. Have you explained to your mom what goes on at youth group? It sounds like *your* youth group is great, but unfortunately, some youth groups are just games and gossip. If your mom thinks you're simply having "recess" with a bunch of other kids at the church, it's understandable why she wouldn't hesitate to keep you home when it's appropriate.

But sit down and explain to her what really goes on. Tell her how youth group is helping you grow in your faith. Share with her what you're learning. And tell her how important it is to you.

Then say something like, "I know I blow it a lot and get grounded, but will you think about grounding me from something other than youth group, because that's sorta like my spiritual vitamins. I really *need* it. Could you ground me from something that's just fun and not something that's fun *and* meaningful—like youth group?"

She may or may not reconsider. In any case, ask God to help you think through the situation before you disobey. This may keep you from getting grounded so often.

Q. My mom has been sick for three weeks, and I've gotta be her servant. She's really cranky, and this is tough! I just want her to get well so things can go back to normal.

A. Hmmm. It sounds as though you want her to get well so "normal" will mean you won't have to do as much around the house. Let's make a short list of some of the things your mom has done for you, okay? I'll get you started; you complete it.

- *She took care of me when I was sick.*
- *She's given me some great birthdays to remember.*
- *She lets me have a friend over to spend the night.*
- *She cooks some great meals!*

-
-
-
-

You've probably done a lot for your mom. But chances are, you haven't done half as much for her in the few years you've lived, as she's done for you. (Not the answer you wanted to hear, huh? Stick with me, okay?)

It could be that she's cranky because of medication. Our bodies react differently to various medicines, and since she's been sick for three weeks, I'm guessing she's probably on a strong prescription.

Chances are, she won't be sick forever. So try to think of this particular time in your life as a *season*. Seasons are only temporary. They come, and they go. I challenge you to look at this as your *giving season*. This is YOUR time to give and give and give to your mom—when she can't give back. (That's the best kind of giving!)

If you'll serve with a cheerful heart, you'll be making incredible memories! And years later, you'll look back on this special season as a unique and wonderful time you were able to do something for your mom that you may never have the opportunity to do again in the same way.

Q. My dad's a pastor and we may be moving to another church in a different state. I'm afraid to leave my friends. Got any advice?

A. I feel for you. It's tough to leave people we love and be the new kid on the block someplace different. But you know what? I'll bet your dad is a little scared, too!

Think about it: *Any* change means adjustment—even *good* changes. And adjustments are hard. So even though your dad may be excited about a new challenge, he's probably a little nervous as well.

Since your dad is a pastor, try to think of this move as a new mission. God is sending you and your family into a brand-new home, school, and church to be his missionaries. We usually think of missionaries as people who live in other countries, but we can be a missionary right where we are!

It's comforting to know that you and your family won't be moving alone—God is going with you. Wow! The Creator of the universe is moving *with* you. Memorize this Scripture for comfort, okay? "And surely I am with you always, to the very end of the age" (Matthew 28:20).

Why don't we pray about your move right now?

Dear Jesus,

I want my dad to follow your leading, but I'm scared. It's hard to leave my friends and go someplace new. Will you teach me to trust you? Strengthen me, Father. Help me to make good friends. In fact, right now—ahead of time—begin preparing the hearts of the girls you've chosen to be my friends.

And thanks, Jesus, for your promise to never leave me.

I love you. Amen.

Q. My grandpa is in the hospital, and I'm scared he's going to die.

A. I remember when *my* grandpa was in the hospital. It's a frightening thing to see someone you love in a hospital bed. We feel out of control, don't we? We want to help, but we don't know what to do.

Here's what will mean the most to your grandpa. Sit by his side. Pray for him out loud. Read the Bible to him (John 14 and 15 are great sections). Gently hold his hand. Smooth his hair. These are wonderful acts of love!

The tough thing about life is the fact that we're *all* eventually going to die physically. But the good news is that we don't have to die spiritually! I hope your grandpa is a Christian. If he's not, ask God to help your grandpa make a spiritual commitment of faith before he dies.

As Christians, we get to live forever (that's a lo-o-o-ong time!) in heaven with our Lord Jesus Christ. That's fantastic news, because the Bible tells us we'll never be sick, or angry, or sad in heaven. Isn't it great that God gives his children something eternal to look forward to?

Q. I don't get enough privacy! I have to wear the key to my diary on a bracelet so my brother and sisters won't read it. What can I do?

A. Sounds like you need to talk with your mom and dad. Your house may not be big enough for you to have your own room. And you probably won't get your own bathroom anytime soon, either. But your diary should be off-limits and your very own personal treasure.

Your parents can help your brother and sisters understand that they're going too far by trying to read your private thoughts.

If that doesn't work, stop writing in your diary for a while. I'll bet after a month or so of having nothing to read, your brother and sisters will forget you even *have* a diary and you can go back to recording your thoughts in it again.

Q. My mom and I don't have a good relationship. I can't talk to her about bras and stuff like that. How can I change it? I feel so shy.

A. Sometimes it's hard to talk about things like bras and having a period and what guy we like, isn't it? That's because all these things are very personal, and it can be embarrassing to ask questions about private things.

But you know what? Your mom is exactly the person who has the answers to all that kind of stuff. I'm serious! She's already had a period, bought a ton of bras, and can probably even remember what it was like to have a crush on the cutest guy in school.

If it's too hard to *talk* about things with her, try keeping a shared journal. I wrote a book called *The Mother/Daughter Connection* that may help you and your mom understand each other better. Ask her if she'd like to read it, and consider getting it for her as a gift.

Q. Both sides of my family have a serious problem with anger. It goes back four or five generations. All of us are always angry! It never goes away. Please help! I'm tired of all the fighting.

A. It's frightening to be around people who are always angry, isn't it? Anger is an emotion, but it's also a behavioral habit that's easy to fall into. For instance, when something doesn't go our way, it's easy to just get angry about it and to continue getting angry whenever we're bothered about something. It can become a habit, and habits are tough to break . . . but not *impossible* to break.

You can't change the generations in your past, but you *can* change your own behavior. This isn't something you can just "will" to happen. It will require a power beyond yourself to change this habit.

This will take the power of God. He doesn't want you to live a life of anger. He wants you to experience joy and peace. In fact, check out what he says in Galatians 5:22–23a: "But the fruit of the Spirit is love, joy, peace, patience, kindness, goodness, faithfulness, gentleness and self-control."

Only God's Holy Spirit can provide the self-control that you need. He also wants to *transform* you. Let's see what the Bible says about that, okay? "Do not conform any longer to the pattern of this world, but be transformed by the renewing of your mind" (Romans 12:2).

Even though everyone in your "world" (your family) is angry and acting out of anger, you don't have to imitate that behavior. Wanna pray about it right now?

Dear Jesus,

It's so hard that my entire family is always angry. I hate it! And it scares me. I'm so glad you understand everything I go through and exactly how I feel.

Jesus, will you transform my mind and my heart? I don't want to copy the angry behavior of my family. I want to be like you. And I want to experience your peace and joy and self-control. Please forgive me for my anger. I'm placing it in your hands right

now. Replace my anger with the fruit of your Holy Spirit.

I realize this will be a process. After all, my relationship with you is a growing one. But help me to keep following you and to read my Bible consistently. Remind me to talk to you throughout my day. I know you'll give me the strength I need to change my behavior.

I love you, Father. Amen.

Questions About Guys

Q. My mom says I can't call boys, and I think that's stupid. What's she so worried about? She knows I'm responsible, but she won't even let me talk for five minutes.

A. Here's the weird thing about growing up: Girls mature more quickly than boys do. This means girls are *usually* interested in boys (wanting a boyfriend, calling them, etc.) before boys are interested in girls.

Your mom knows this . . . which also means she knows that you're either going to call a boy who really isn't interested in talking on the phone with you (and *ouch!* that's gonna be embarrassing to *you*) or you'll call a boy who's older and *is* interested in girls.

I encourage you to stay away from older boys who are looking for a younger girlfriend. At your age, it's best to remain friends with those close to your age. I've known boys in your age bracket who absolutely hate it when girls call their house. They're just not interested in girls yet; they don't want to talk on the phone; they don't know *how* to carry on a conversation with a girl. And what happens? They begin to dislike the girl, and her feelings are crushed.

Again, your mom knows all this. She probably also knows that in the long run, you'd much rather be pursued than be the pursuer. (In other words, wouldn't it feel better to have a guy showing interest in you, instead of you having to be the one trying to "catch" him?)

In a few years, guys will start calling *you* and your mom will more than likely allow you to talk on the phone with them. Until then? Ask your mom to explain her reasons to you and try to learn as much as you can from her.

Q. Our school had a dance last week, and I danced with one of my good guy friends. Afterward, he acted like it was no big deal, but to me it was a big deal! I enjoyed it, and I like him a lot. Why did he act like that? And why do I feel this way? I'm so confused!

A. Guys and girls are so different—not only physically, but emotionally, too! We girls often tend to "fall" for a guy faster than he "falls" for us. We're more emotional by nature. We love the romance of the moment, and guys love the action.

Does that mean no guys are romantics? No. I'm making some generalized statements—in other words, I'm speaking in terms of what *often* happens, not what *always* happens.

This particular guy may not even be interested yet in anything more than a friendship with a girl. But he was at a dance, and he did what people do at dances— he danced! That doesn't mean he's interested in you. Neither does it mean he doesn't like you as a friend. So why did he "act like this"? I'm guessing he's not acting at all. He's probably just not ready for any kind of guy/girl thing yet.

But while you were dancing, you were feeling the romance of the moment. He was probably thinking about not stepping on your feet and wondering why he's sweating so much.

Slow down! Right now concentrate simply on being a good friend to everyone—guys *and* girls.

Q. *I'm only twelve, so I know I'm too young to date. But what is the right age?*

A. That's a tough one. We know the right age to drive—sixteen. And we know the voting age is twenty-one. But when it comes to dating, it gets a little more complicated. Why? Because everyone matures at different rates.

I know some twelve-year-old girls who are way more responsible than some sixteen-year-olds. And I know some fourteen-year-old gals who are more mature than seventeen-year-olds. Yet it's usually the older girls who are dating, isn't it?

Since your mom probably knows you better than anyone else, she's a great person to ask about when you'll be ready to date. Ask her what she wants to see in you before she will give the go-ahead to date. Are you dependable in getting your chores done? Responsible to turn your homework in on time and get back videos and library books before they're overdue? When she says no to something you want to do, how do you react?

Your reactions in these situations tell your mom a lot about your emotional maturity. I guarantee if you're not being responsible in the home, she'll think you won't be responsible outside of the home.

I suggest you jot down all your questions about dating and ask Mom for an evening the two of you can spend together. Bring your list of questions and discuss it with her. (The key word here is *discuss*—which is totally different than arguing.) I'll give you some examples of questions you can ask, and you come up with some of your own, okay?

- *What is dating?*
- *When did you have your first date?*
- *Will you tell me about it?*
- *How old should I be when I begin dating?*
- *What are some qualities I should be able to see in a guy I date?*
- *What guy qualities were important to you when you were dating?*
-

Q. I wanna talk to this guy at school, but I just can't! I get all tongue-tied when he walks by.

A. And your heart probably beats a little faster, too, huh? It can be scary to start a conversation with someone you're not used to talking with. Here's what I suggest: Find out what he's interested in. If he plays baseball, talk about that. Say something like, "I saw you playing baseball yesterday. You're really good."

If he's into computers, ask him about it: "What kind of computer software do you have?"

If he did a good job on an oral report in class, comment on it. "I enjoyed your report. You made the book sound so interesting, I'm thinking about reading it."

If you can't find out what he's interested in, start with just saying hi and smiling. Do that for a few days straight. Then add a little to it: "Hi. How's it goin'?" Do that for a few days.

Then add to *that:* "Hey, cool shirt. You know, we see each other a lot, but I'm not sure we really know each other. My name is . . ."

Eventually, you'll begin to feel more confident about talking with him. But start slow and don't expect to carry on an entire conversation the first time you talk. Build up to it.

Q. I've liked this boy I've known since kindergarten. When I'm with him my stomach does flip-flops. He chases every girl in sight — except me. How can I get him to notice me?

A. Are you sure you're interested in someone who's "chasing every girl in sight"? That doesn't sound very special. I encourage you to be nice to him but shift your interests elsewhere.

If you don't want to follow that advice, think about this: What are you currently doing to try to get his attention? It could be you're trying too hard. Many guys want something that's not easy to get. In other words, they enjoy "the hunt." To have to go after a girl can be fun and adventurous to them. If a girl is too easy to catch, there's no challenge for him.

Again, be nice to him. Talk with him. Ask him questions about what his hobbies are. But don't just always be there when he turns around. If you make yourself a little more scarce, he may become more interested in you.

Q. This guy at school likes me. At break and during lunch we hold hands a lot. I don't really like him that much, but I don't want to hurt his feelings. How do I get out of holding his hand?

A. *Yikes!* Holding hands with a guy just because you don't want to hurt his feelings isn't a good reason to hold hands. When you hold someone's hand, it should be very special. It should be because you care deeply about him. Be very selective about whose hands you choose to hold.

Why? Because when you hold hands, you're automatically giving a guy a message—the "I like you" message. You're not being fair to him by sending him a message that's not true.

So tell him how you feel; but be gentle and kind. Let's practice right here, okay? I'll jot down a couple of examples of what you can say to him, and you create a few of your own.

- *"We've been holding hands a lot, and I'm beginning to think maybe we're going too fast. Let's back up, okay?"*
- *"You know . . . I'm not sure if I'm really ready for a boyfriend right now. Let's just be friends."*
- *"You're a great guy. I like you a lot . . . but I'd rather just be your friend instead of your girlfriend."*
-
-
-
-

Q. *I like this really, really, really cute boy at school, but he likes another girl. What should I do?*

A.   Nothing—except be nice to him *and* the girl he likes. Turn it around in your mind for a second. What if you were the girl he liked but another girl wanted to divert his attention from you to her?

It would hurt deeply, wouldn't it? Don't make that mistake. Trust God with *all* your friendships—and yep, that includes guys *and* girls.

Questions About Body and Health

Q. I'm so frustrated! I wash my face twice a day, and it still breaks out!

A. You're not alone! There's probably no one in the entire world who hasn't struggled with facial blemishes. But you're on the right track! Washing your face daily is the most important thing you can do for your complexion.

Between ages eleven and twenty-one, your pores become easily clogged because your hormones are changing. That's why it's so helpful to keep your face clean. But since you're already doing that, you may need a little extra help. Ask your mom if she'll make an appointment for you with a dermatologist (a physician who's trained to work specifically with skin problems).

He can give you a prescription for medicated lotion that should help heal your breakouts.

Q. My teeth look totally gross. They're small and yellow. I'm not too worried about them being small, but I hate the fact that they're yellow. I brush my teeth three times every day, and I've tried whitening toothpaste, but it hasn't worked.

Is there anything I can do that isn't expensive and can be done at home to make my teeth white?

I'm so self-conscious about them, I don't even want to smile.

A. We all have something we wish we could change about ourselves—our nose is too big, we're too tall, too short, etc. And for whatever reason, some people have teeth that are more yellow or gray than most. I'm wondering if you've asked your dentist about some whitening products. There are some teeth bleaching agents and even dental paint that can be used to whiten teeth.

When I was five years old, our family doctor prescribed some medicine for me that permanently stained my teeth. So I've lived with darker teeth than most people for years. I tried bleaching them, and I had a dentist who tried painting them. But the only thing that *totally* worked was when I got porcelain crowns put on six of my front teeth this year. Now I finally have white teeth!

You're probably not dealing with a permanent stain (that particular medicine was taken off the market when they found out what it did to teeth!), and you may still have some baby teeth that you'll lose. So I encourage you to talk with your dentist. Tell him how often you're brushing, and ask what he recommends you use for whitening.

Q. *I'm concerned about my health. I know I don't eat right—because it's usually junk food. Do you think I should go on a diet? And do you have any fun ideas on how I can get a little exercise every day?*

A. I admire you for wanting to improve your health. That's terrific! Before you begin dieting, though, ask your mom about it first. You're right in the middle of some very important years. During this specific time, your body is changing and growing. Your muscles are developing, and your hormones are waking up. Sometimes dieting during the preteen and teen years can actually do more harm than good.

I suggest instead of really going on a diet, you simply try to make wiser food choices. For example, when you're hungry don't grab a bag of chips. Go for some carrots. When you're thirsty, stay away from Coca-Cola and drink water instead. Your mom can help you with some healthy food options.

I'm excited that you want to exercise. The key to staying consistent with an exercise plan is to find something you enjoy. Do you like to rollerblade? How about walking? Are you into jump rope? Whatever it is you enjoy, do *that!* I know some young girls who absolutely love to jump rope. They love it so much, they decided to create some jump rope chants to say while they jump. And guess what! They're in the process now of getting their jump rope chants published into a book!

If you enjoy walking, use this time to talk to God as you walk. If you have a dog, take him with you. And, of course, it's always more fun to exercise with a friend. Can you find someone to walk, play tennis, ride bikes, or skate with you? If not, go ahead and do it on your own. You'll be surprised at how much better you'll feel when you exercise.

Q. Some of my friends are starting to wear makeup. My mom said I can wear a little too. But I don't know how to put it on, and I feel really stupid having to ask someone. Help!

A. Please don't feel stupid. Applying makeup is something that has to be learned; no one is born knowing how to do it. And the more you practice, the better you'll get at it.

You've probably noticed there are several makeup counters in some of the bigger stores in the mall. Ask your mom if she'll make an appointment for you at one of the counters that sell makeup products. They'll put you in a special chair and teach you how to apply makeup. They can also tell which shades look best on you and how much you need.

A common mistake with a lot of beginners is putting on too much makeup. The goal isn't to pile it on; that only makes you look made-up and fake. The goal is to look natural by using makeup to enhance—or bring out—the beauty you already have.

Q. I want to lose weight really bad. Everyone's getting new swimsuits for summer, and I'm feeling desperate to get thinner!

A. At your age, I don't really think dieting is important. It's better to get plenty of exercise—at least twenty minutes four times a week—and to eat healthy. In other words, stay away from the Twinkies and french fries and try to eat more veggies and baked or grilled chicken.

Q. I've always heard that we should drink six to eight glasses of water every day. But why?

A. The reason it's important to drink so much water is because it helps keep us "flushed out." In other words, water aids your body in getting rid of all the stuff it doesn't need.

Q. *People make fun of all the hair on my arms. I'm so desperate, I'm thinking about shaving it off. I'm tired of their remarks!*

A. Please *don't!* If you shave it off, it won't grow back the same. It may grow in crooked or even thicker than it is now. God made you just the way you are, and he wants you to feel good about how you look.

Your friends may not have as much hair on their arms as you do, but I'll bet there's *something* each wishes she could change about her looks. And that's the problem: When we compare ourselves to those around us, we're only setting ourselves up for disappointment.

I know it's hard to believe, but by the time you're out of college, you probably won't care or even think about the hair on your arms. Right now you're still under construction. Your body will continue to change during the next few years.

Ask God to help you love yourself just the way you are. And when people make fun of your arms, you have two choices: Either laugh *with* them (it's okay to laugh at yourself), or tell them those kind of comments really hurt.

Rest assured that Jesus Christ knows exactly how you feel. When you hurt, he hurts. Why don't we talk to him about it right now?

Dear Jesus,
I get so tired of people making fun of the way I look! Thanks for knowing how I

feel and for really caring about how hurt I am! The Bible says that you made me in your own image. I know that's special . . . but I don't feel special right now.

Please help me see myself through your eyes and not my own. Teach me how to like myself. I'm going to trust you with my appearance, Jesus.

I love you. Amen.

Q. I have large pores on my face. Is there a way to make them not so noticeable?

A. Check with some of the makeup counters at the bigger stores in the mall to see if they have a product called pore-minimizer makeup. Get the clear skin formula. If you apply it before putting on any makeup, it'll help decrease the appearance of your facial pores.

Q. I'm hungry a lot, but I don't want to snack on junk food all the time. Any suggestions for some healthy snacks?

A. There's probably a good reason you're so hungry. Are you active? Are you involved in sports? Do you play outside and expend a lot of energy? Are you always on the go?

Even if you're *not* physically active, your body is right in the midst of a bunch of changes right now, and sometimes that can make a person hungry. I think it's cool that you want to snack on something healthy instead of reaching for the cupcakes.

I suggest you head to the library or a bookstore and find a book that will give you some healthy snack ideas. You could even invite several of your girlfriends over for an evening of snack making. There are all kinds of healthy *and* tasty fruit smoothies you can make, along with some veggies and great dip. Make a party out of it!

Q. *I overheard some teen girls talking about their 'colors'. What does this mean?*

A. Knowing your "colors" means finding out what colors look best on you. Colors are broken down into two major categories—warm and cool. Warm colors all have a yellowish undertone, and cool colors all have a bluish-pink undertone.

Underneath those two major categories, there are four divisions that are broken down into the four seasons—autumn, spring, summer, and winter. Autumn and spring are considered sister seasons and are composed of warm colors. Summer and winter are sister seasons and are made up of cool colors.

Let's use the color green for an example. A winter person would look best wearing emerald green. A summer person would want to wear blue-green. Someone who's a spring person would wear kelly green, and an autumn person would look best in olive green.

If you're interested in finding out your colors, talk with a beauty consultant (several large department stores have them). Or visit a bookstore and ask for a book that has some sample color charts.

Q. A few days ago I cut my bangs. Now they're too short. (I mean, they're really short!) I look stupid! What can I do?

A. The only good thing about a bad haircut is about four weeks! In other words, your hair *will* grow back— it just takes a while. Meantime, consider wearing some fun hats or headbands. And if you get the urge to cut your hair again . . . don't!

Q. What's puberty? And how will I know when I'm going through it?

A. Puberty is when your body begins changing from a little girl into a young woman. You've probably heard about girls having a menstrual cycle (a monthly period), and your breasts will begin to grow. You'll also become more interested in boys.

How will you know when it hits? You'll actually see some of the changes happening to your body. You'll grow hair under your arms and around your vagina. Of course, you won't be able to see the changes going on *inside* your body, but you'll know something is happening.

Don't be frightened. Puberty—or growing up—happens to everyone. It's totally natural. If you have questions, though, don't be embarrassed to ask your mom. After all, she's already gone through it and can tell you what to expect.

Q. Most of the girls in my class are beginning to grow breasts. When will mine start to grow?

A. Since everyone matures at a different rate, it's impossible to know exactly when you'll start to change physically. But girls can usually expect breast development to happen anytime between the ages of nine and sixteen.

When your breasts *do* begin to grow, you might notice some soreness in that area. That's okay. You're normal. You'll also want to talk with your mom about getting your first bra.

Q. I wanna do something new and totally different with my hair. But I don't have a clue where to start.

A. Look through a variety of magazines and cut out the pictures of styles you like. Also, ask your mom if she'll take you to talk with a hairstylist. A stylist can give you several suggestions just by looking at you in her chair and swiveling you around and feeling the texture of your hair. She'll also take the shape of your face into consideration and suggest something that will look good on you.

Stylists usually have several magazines or books you can look through to get ideas on specific styles.

Q. I really want a tan, but my mom says I'll get skin cancer if I stay out in the sun too long. What can I do?

A. Guess what—your mom is right! I went to the dermatologist (a skin doctor) who removed a little bump from my arm, and I couldn't help noticing all the photos of skin cancer in his waiting room. It was really scary!

Did you know that your skin stores every single bit of sunlight you're exposed to? For instance, when you played outside all day, every day during the summer after third grade, you got a lot of sun. Your body still has that radiation. And even when you walk from your house to the car, your body picks up the sun's radiation and stores it. So yeah, this skin cancer stuff is serious!

But the good news is that you can still get a tan. There are several sunless tanning lotions and gels on the market. You may look "streaked" for two or three days, but afterward it evens out and looks like a natural tan. You can find the less expensive ones at your local grocery or discount store, and you can purchase the higher-cost gels and creams at any beauty counter in the mall.

Q. My breasts are two totally different sizes. I'm so embarrassed. I just wanna be normal! What's wrong with me? I feel like a freak!

A. Relax! You're normal. Breasts don't grow at the same speed, so your right one might be a little bigger than your left one. But eventually they'll catch up with one another and even out. You're not a freak—you're just in the middle of growing and changing. It's okay. I promise. *No* girl's breasts grow together at the same rate.

Q. Whenever I wear a ponytail during the day, I have a ring the next day where the ponytail holder was the day before. I don't keep my ponytail in during the night, so I'd think that little bulge would go away, but it doesn't!

A. Hmmm. Sounds like you're not washing your hair the next morning. If you'll wash your hair when you get up in the morning, the bulge will automatically disappear.

Q. *Some people in our church say that wearing makeup isn't Christian.*

A. They might be basing their opinion on this Scripture: "I also want women to dress modestly, with decency and propriety, not with braided hair or gold or pearls or expensive clothes, but with good deeds, appropriate for women who profess to worship God" (1 Timothy 2:9–10).

If we do a little biblical research, we'll discover that the apostle Paul wrote this letter to Timothy—a young pastor leading the church in Ephesus. Before we chat about the makeup issue, let's unpack some background on this whole situation, okay? There were several false teachers trying to confuse the folks in Timothy's church, and these false teachers were specifically targeting the women there.

Things had gotten out of control, and women were standing up in the middle of a church service and talking loudly. Obviously this was a huge distraction. That's why Paul wrote in 1 Timothy 2:11 for the women to be silent. In this particular church, they *needed* to be silent! Sometimes people read this Scripture today and assume that Paul hated women. But that's not true. Up to this point, women hadn't even been allowed in the church services, so Paul and the new Christians were making great strides in helping women join in on everything.

These false teachers were preying on the women, and Timothy needed advice on how to protect them. So when Paul wrote in 1 Timothy 2:12 not to let women teach or have positions in the church, he was trying to get them out of the public eye of the false teachers; in other words, he was looking out for them.

There are other places in Scripture that show Paul's admiration for female teachers and recognition of the importance of women in spreading the Gospel (Romans 16:1–3; Philippians 4:2–3).

Okay, now that you understand what was happening in Timothy's church, and why Paul wrote what he did, let's get to the issue of makeup.

In this specific church (the Ephesian church), lots of jewelry, fancy whipped-up hairdos, and extravagant clothing were a distraction to the worshipers. Those who were distracted complained to Pastor Timothy. Again, because he was young, the older and wiser apostle Paul wrote to give him advice. He simply told him to teach the women in his church not to be concerned with fancy hair, makeup, jewelry, and expensive clothing.

So does that mean jewelry, styled hair, makeup, and expensive clothes are wrong? I don't think so. I don't think God cares as much about the *style* you're wearing as he does the *distraction*.

So think about it: How are you dressing? If you're wearing tons of makeup and jewelry, you may distract someone from what the pastor is saying. I think if I saw a girl come into my church with fuchsia eye makeup, a half pound of thick foundation and blush, twenty-eight bracelets, and an expensive fur coat during the summer, I'd be a little distracted. God doesn't care if this gal wears all this stuff. But he *does* care if she wears it in a situation that's going to keep those around her from growing spiritually.

I don't believe there's anything wrong with wearing makeup, jewelry, or getting your hair styled. That's all part of looking our best. It's when we overdo it that distraction sets in.

The key? Balance. If Jesus is truly Lord of your life, you'll allow him to guide every single area of your life— including what you wear and where you wear it.

Q. I can't figure out why my best friend's elbows are really soft and mine are really rough. My knees are rough, too.

A. Maybe you just have tougher skin than she does. Put lotion on your elbows and knees every morning and every night. That will help keep them soft.

Q. What do you think about getting a tattoo? An older girl at my school got one and everyone's saying how cool it looks.

A. I think it would be a mistake. Once you get a tattoo, that's it—it's permanent. Well ... there *is* a method of "tattoo removal," but it's extremely painful and incredibly expensive and doesn't always work.

Though it might seem like the cool thing to do right now, try to imagine how you'll feel when you're older and your grandkids are wondering why there's a snake on your leg.

Okay, maybe you wouldn't get a snake, but I think you get my point. You may want it now, but most people who get tattooed in their preteen and teen years regret it later.

Q. When will I start my period? I'm kinda embarrassed to admit this ... but I'm scared. Will it hurt?

A. Hey, it's okay to be scared. Most people *are* frightened of something they don't understand. But once you understand what your period is and how it happens, you probably won't be scared at all.

Having a period won't hurt, but you might get some lower abdominal cramps, and those can hurt a bit. I suggest you talk with your mom (after all, she's been having a period for a lo-o-o-ong time!), and ask her to explain how and why it happens.

If you don't have a mom who will do that, think about getting a book from the library about the menstrual cycle. It's really no big deal—just your body's way of first releasing an egg and then blood every month that it doesn't need. But the cool thing is that having a period means you're turning into a young woman. It's your body's way of preparing itself to someday carry a baby!

Q. I've had my period for almost a year now, but I cramp really bad. Last month I was in tears.

A. Cramps are really common and really frustrating! Drink lots of water during your period. Why is that important? Well, cramps are caused by little blood clots, and the water will wash out those blood clots.

Know what else will help? Some light exercise. Try walking around the block or down to the corner. Also, talk to your mom about using some over-the-counter painkillers that have ibuprofen in them.

Q. My period is irregular. I'll have it one month—then I'll skip a couple of months—and I'll have it again.

A. And I'm guessing that sometimes it lasts for a whole week and other times it's gone after four days, right? That's okay. It's normal for a girl's period to be irregular during the first two or three years. If it's irregular for years on end, you'll want to make an appointment with your doctor just to make sure everything's okay.

Q. How come I always feel fat when I have my period?

A. That's because your body will tend to retain water during this time. So slack off on salty foods and soft drinks that contain caffeine.

Q. I get razor burn when I shave. Am I doing something wrong?

A. Are you trying to shave dry legs? If so, that may be the cause. Try soaking your legs in warm water before you shave, and don't push hard with your razor. It also helps to use a shaving foam or gel. When you've finished shaving, apply lotion or baby oil to your legs.

Q. How can I keep my nails from splitting and breaking?

A. First of all, make sure you're getting enough protein in your diet. If you're not, this could cause your nails to weaken and break. If you don't want to wear colored nail polish, use a clear polish as a coating over your nails. This will help keep them shielded and keep them from cracking so easily.

Q. I have a scar on my arm, and I'm self-conscious about it. Is there anything I can do to make it less noticeable?

A. It may *feel* like everyone is looking at or noticing your scar, but I'll bet they really aren't. I remember getting a huge zit on my nose when I was in high school. I was absolutely positive every single person in the world was focusing on it. I was even embarrassed to go to church and Sunday school that morning. But when I arrived, no one said anything and they treated me as they always did. It taught me that when I don't like something about my body, I notice it more than others do.

Check with the pharmacist at your local drugstore for some Vitamin E. That's been helpful in making scars less noticeable. Though you'd rather *not* have a scar on your arm, it's okay. You're still just as beautiful and valuable as ever!

Q. My hair is fine and thick. Whenever I style it, it always goes flat — even when I use hair spray or mousse. How can I keep it styled?

A. Sounds like you could use a haircut that has some layers to it. A hairstylist can layer your hair so that it has some body and will stay styled for longer periods of time.

Q. I put makeup on every time I go somewhere, but I still don't feel pretty! And when I was angry, I cut my hair really short. When will it grow past my shoulders again? Help! I want to be attractive. What can I do?

A. Okay, let's start with the anger. Never do anything rash or spontaneous when you're angry. Make yourself wait a day or two before you get a haircut, spend your money, or make that big decision. When will your hair grow past your shoulders? That depends on how short you cut it. It'll take a while, and you're just going to have to wait it out.

Now let's chat about you not feeling pretty. Believe it or not, makeup really can't make *anyone* pretty. Real beauty comes from within. If you like yourself, it shows! And if you like yourself, it's easier for others to like you as well.

Think about it: We're all attracted to people who are fun and confident and laugh and smile—not someone who's always worried about how she looks. Know what a girl's most important feature is? Her smile! That's right. Make yourself smile even when you don't feel like it.

See, being attractive can become a personality trait. Ask God to help you develop a healthy, strong, positive self-image. (Self-image is how we see ourselves.) When you truly like yourself, you seem attractive to other people. A friend of mine wrote a book that I think you'd love. It's called *God Thinks You're Positively Awesome!* by Andrea Stephens (Servant Publishers). Check your local Christian bookstore for a copy.

But right now, let's talk to God about your feelings, okay?

Dear Father,
I don't feel very pretty. And when I don't feel pretty, I don't like myself. Please for-

give me for not liking me. I know you created me in love and in your image. Teach me
how to love myself like you love me.

Jesus, help me to smile and be kind to
people even when I don't feel like it. And
help my feelings to eventually catch up to
those actions.

I love you, Father. I'm going to start
spending more time reading my Bible and
talking with you. Because I know the more
I do that, the more you'll be able to help me
love myself.

Amen.

Section Four

Questions About Friends

Q. My friend's dad got really mad at her because she didn't make first chair in band. I'm glad my dad isn't like that. But I feel badly for her. How can I help?

A. I'm glad your dad isn't like that, too. No one needs that kind of pressure. Unfortunately, some parents try to get their kids to do stuff that they always wanted to do during their own childhood but never did. It's not fair to try and relive those areas of interest through your children.

The best thing you can do for your friend is to simply continue being her friend and pray for her. Affirm her in the things she does well—even if they're small things. For instance, does she have good handwriting? Tell her. She has a beautiful smile? Let her know. You like what she's wearing? Compliment her.

She may not get much affirmation at home, so it would be great if she can get it from you and your family. Ask your parents if you can invite her for dinner. It will help her to be around a positive family who accepts and loves her just like she is.

Q. My best friend told me she shoplifted some lip-stick and nail polish! I couldn't believe it! What should I do?

A. Confront her. Get in her face about it. What she did was not only against the law, but she sinned as well. Let her know that you don't approve of her behavior. Stress that stealing—no matter how big or small the item—is always wrong!

Tell her you think she ought to return the lipstick and nail polish to the store manager and apologize for what she did. If she refuses, talk with your parents about it.

Q. One of my friends isn't really my friend any more. My mom told me to 'kill her with kind-ness'. So I did. Well, that didn't help at all. She tore up the school photo I had given her, and she put it in my locker.

I've talked with our school counselor, and that helped a little, but this girl is really being mean to me. Today she cussed me out.

You know that old saying, 'Sticks and stones can break my bones, but words can never harm me?' Well, I've learned it's wrong. Words do hurt! Got any ideas on how I can get through this?

A. Wow! You're really hurting. I'm so sorry you're going through such a hard time with this girl. She doesn't sound like a friend at *all* to me.

Ask God to bring to your mind anything you may have done to hurt her. If he reveals something to you, write her a letter and mail it to her house (since she tore up the last thing you gave her, you may have better luck with actual mail).

If God doesn't bring anything to your mind, and you honestly don't think you've done anything, back off. Continue to smile when you pass her in the hall, but don't go out of your way to try and befriend her. She's making it very clear she doesn't want to be your friend anymore. Respect that and keep your distance.

There are probably several other girls who would love to be your friend—a *real* friend.

Q. I have a tough time explaining to my friends why I don't go to PG—13

movies or watch suggestive TV shows.
How can I help them understand my
standards?

A. Maybe you've heard the phrase "garbage in/ garbage out." Explain to your friends that if we sit around watching violent movies and TV shows all the time, violence will show up in our lives. Not immediately, but at some point we'll become angry and maybe even abusive.

You may be aware of the violence that's been happening in schools around the nation. Most of those young killers played hours and hours of violent video games, listened to violent music, and watched violent movies.

But . . . you may never get them to understand your values! But that's okay. We don't have high standards *only* if our friends approve or understand. We have high standards because we have a high calling on our lives. God has called us to holiness—and that means saying no to some things non-Christians don't find wrong—and that includes movies containing sexual immorality and violence.

Q. My best friend keeps doing everything with another girl. I've already told her how I feel, and it didn't help at all. Should I not have a best friend?

A. There's absolutely nothing wrong with wanting to hang out with those whom we "click" with. The problem comes when we begin to exclude others. There's not a worse feeling in the world than being left out, is there?

The interesting thing about friendships during your preteen and teen years is that they'll shift and change a lot. You may be really tight with Jamie when you're ten, but by the time you're twelve you may hardly ever see her. That's natural. Friendships weave and wind different directions. That doesn't mean you don't *like* Jamie anymore. It simply means your interests and friends have changed.

That's probably what's happening with your friend. She's probably just wanting to branch out and make *more* friends. That's okay. Let her. Don't cling to her— that will only make her feel trapped. Continue to be nice to her but also make new friends.

While it's fun to call someone your "best friend," my advice is simply to be nice to *everyone.* Be friends with as many people as you can. That way, you can't lose!

Q. People at school gossip about me. Help! It really hurts.

A. *Ouch!* You're right; it *does* hurt when people talk about us in a negative way. If you were here, we'd go out for a big ol' Cherry Coke and just unload. But since we're not together, let's just chat through the page inside this book, okay?

This may be hard to think about . . . but here goes: Are you doing anything to prompt the gossip? Before we talk about how to deal with hurtful gossip, let's do a little soul-searching first.

For instance, if people are saying you're stuck-up, it could be that you're ignoring classmates without even realizing it. If they're saying you brag, listen to your own conversation . . . do you talk about yourself a lot?

In other words, listen first, then search your heart. If what they're saying is totally untrue—and you're not doing anything to bring it on—follow a powerful strategy.

What strategy? Here it is: *Pray for them.* Yeah, I know that's hard to read. But you know what? The more you pray for those who are hurting you, the more God helps you love them. And when you can truly love those who are hurting you, they can't help but notice.

Q. *One of my friends calls me on the phone all the time. I like talking on the phone, but she just sits there! I don't wanna be rude, but I hate listening to silence.*

 A. Here are a few ideas:

- *Ask your mom to limit your phone calls with this girl. After three minutes you can say, "Gotta go. Mom said so."*
- *Don't force the conversation. If she doesn't say something, you've probably been jumping in and filling the silence. Go ahead and listen to the*

silence for a few minutes. This will hopefully force her to say something.

- *When she calls, cheerfully say, "Hi! What do you wanna talk about?" If she says, "Nothing," or "I don't know," then you can respond with, "Okay. Well, call me back when you wanna talk." Hopefully, she'll pick up the hint that conversation is a two-way thing and she needs to do her part to keep one going. If she doesn't take a hint, you may just need to say, "I love talking on the phone, but I feel weird when you don't say anything. If we're gonna talk, you've gotta say stuff."*

Q. I have a friend at church who always talks during the service. I like her a lot, but her talking disturbs me and those around me. It's really hard to get anything out of our pastor's sermon when my friend is always talking.

The thing is, I want to listen; I don't wanna talk during church, but I don't know what to do about it. If I sit with someone else, her feelings will get hurt. What can I do?

A. In the Old Testament, we have a list of the Ten Commandments. (You can read them in Exodus 20:1–17.) Guess what commandment six says: "You shall not murder."

When we think of killing someone, we usually think of a physical murder. But there's another way to kill someone, and that's by *spiritually* murdering him or her.

Your friend probably doesn't realize it, but she could be spiritually killing those around her. She's keeping them from hearing God's voice through your pastor and the music and everything else that's designed to help us worship him during a church service.

I realize you don't want to hurt her feelings, and that is good. But for once you have to put those good intentions aside. The important thing in this situation is that you get to listen and grow spiritually while you're in church. Gently explain to her that more than anything you really want to grow closer to God and listen to what your pastor is saying.

She may not realize how much she's talking. Tell her you'd love to continue sitting with her if she'll be respectful of those around her and not talk. Maybe she's talking because she's bored. Challenge her to take notes on what the pastor is saying. Then the two of you can compare your notes after church. If she still can't respect your wishes, you can kindly explain to her that you'll sit somewhere else during church and hang out with her afterward.

Q. My friend is suddenly ignoring me, and I can't figure out why! It totally hurts.

A. The best way to patch things up with a friend is to talk with her. You may have done or said something that hurt her feelings. Ask her. If she says that you haven't, then tell her you're feeling ignored and left out. Explain how much you care about her friendship and that you're hurting.

She may be going through a tough time at home. Maybe she's afraid her parents are going to split up, or perhaps her brother's messing around with drugs. She may be so preoccupied with family problems that she might not even realize she's ignoring you.

But you'll never know until you talk to her. So give her a call right now, okay?

Q. *A girl at my school doesn't eat lunch; she only drinks a Coke. How can I help? Should I say anything?*

A. I'm proud of you for caring! I hope you'll reach out to her and befriend her. Ask her to eat at your table. Offer to share your lunch with her. If she refuses, pack two sandwiches tomorrow and say, "Hey! I've got two sandwiches. I don't want two. Can you eat one for me? Please? I don't wanna toss it in the can."

You may have heard of anorexia and bulimia. They're dangerous eating disorders that can eventually kill a person. Anorexia is starving yourself to death, and bulimia is eating tons of food and trying to get rid of it by vomiting or other means. Eating disorders are nothing to mess around with!

But before we assume this girl has an eating disorder, let's look at another possibility. Maybe she doesn't have any money. If her family is low on cash, she may be embarrassed to ask for meal coupons and is just trying to get by with only drinking something.

I encourage you to tell a teacher. A school counselor or teacher can privately find out if she needs money, or if it's something else.

Q. My friend's birthday is coming up soon, and I can't think of anything to get her. Got any good ideas?

A. Sure, I'll start you off with a few, and you complete the list, okay?

- *A cool CD with fun Christian music. (How about Plus One, Rebecca St. James, Jake, Shine, dc Talk?)*
- *A fun video of the two of you. (You'll need to borrow a video camera if your family doesn't have one. Take turns filming each other doing wacky stuff. Grab your mom or dad and ask them to film both of you swinging in the park, giggling, eating ice cream, etc.) She can watch it whenever she needs a bright spot in a dreary day.*
- *A stack of custom-made greeting cards. (Go to a craft store and get supplies to make your own cards. Create a set of 12 for her—everything from birthday cards, Christmas cards, congratulations cards, etc. that she can send to her friends and family members.)*

- *A few bottles of wild and crazy nail polish. (You'll have fun polishing each other's toenails in neon green!)*

-

-

-

Questions About Faith

Q. How do I know if I'm really a Christian?

A. Have you confessed your sins and asked Christ to forgive you? Have you given your life to him? Are you obeying him and following him? If so, you're a Christian. Salvation is a gift. There's absolutely nothing you can do to earn it. And you'll never be good enough to deserve it. God wants to forgive your sins through Jesus Christ, simply because he loves you!

Salvation is like a Christmas gift. Someone may present you with a beautifully wrapped box, complete with fancy bow and ribbons. Even though they hold it out to you and it has your name on the tag, it doesn't really become yours until you accept it.

It works the same way spiritually. God wants you to accept salvation—his forgiveness of your sins. He's offering it free.

Check this out: "This righteousness from God comes through faith in Jesus Christ to all who believe.... All have sinned and fall short of the glory of God, and are justified freely by his grace through the redemption that came by Christ Jesus" (Romans 3:22–24).

If you've never asked Christ to forgive your sins, and if you've never given your life to him, you're not a Christian. Being good and going to church doesn't make you a Christian. Wanna pray right now?

Dear Jesus,

I realize I was born a sinner. I'm sorry for my sinful life, Father. I've been selfish, and I've done things that have made you sad. Will you forgive me? Will you come into my life and make me a brand-new person in your name?

I want to live for you, Jesus. I believe you died for my sins and rose from the dead and are preparing a place for me right now in heaven to live forever with you after I die. I also believe that the Bible is your Holy Word. I believe it is absolute Truth.

Thank you so much for granting me forgiveness for my sins. Jesus, I don't deserve this *kind of supernatural love, but I sure am grateful for it. Help me to read the Bible and grow closer to you. I'm placing you in charge of my life, and I will live in obedience to you. Amen.*

Guess what! If you prayed that prayer and meant it, you're a Christian. The Bible tells us that when someone becomes a Christian, all of heaven rejoices! So right now there's a party going on in heaven because of your commitment to Jesus Christ. Cool, huh?

But this is just the beginning. That prayer isn't an automatic ticket to heaven. That prayer is the beginning of a beautiful relationship God wants to establish with you. And a relationship takes action. You wouldn't be able to keep up a friendship with your best friend if you never talked to her or spent any time together, would you? Well, it works the same way with God. Read your Bible. Pray. Get to know him. He wants to be your very best Friend.

If you don't attend church, find one. Get involved in a Bible study and a youth group. This will help you grow stronger spiritually. You might want to ask your pastor about baptizing you. This is a wonderful way to tell others about your commitment to Jesus.

Q. I love God, and I'm a Christian. But I think church is really boring! Does this mean I'm a bad Christian?

A. No, you're not a bad Christian—you're just bored. Guess what—I get bored sometimes, too! Some of us just don't have a long attention span (like me!), and it's easy for our minds to wander. But I've found a little trick that helps keep me interested and tuned in to what's going on: I take notes!

In fact, our church even has some special notebooks that we can use. This makes it easy for me to remember what the sermon was about after church is over. I can refer to my notes and keep thinking about the message during the week.

Here's what I suggest:

- *Take notes on the pastor's sermon.*
- *Sit close to the front so you won't be distracted.*
- *Arrive early and ask God to help you keep your mind focused. Ask him to teach you something today through this particular church service.*
- *Discuss the service with your family or friends afterward. (This will help you keep thinking about it, enable you to ask questions about anything you didn't understand, and apply it to your own life.)*

Q. *I think I'm a good Christian, but I hardly ever go to church. Well ... I go to church events—like our New Year's Eve party and the annual lockin. Is this wrong?*

A. It's not *wrong*, but it's not *wise*. Is there a reason you're not going to church? If you truly want to grow closer to Christ, there are some specific things you need to do:

- *Read your Bible consistently.*
- *Pray (talk to Jesus) often.*
- *Become involved in your local church and youth group.*

Why is this last thing so important? Because it helps us to be surrounded by other growing Christians. We grow and learn from their testimonies. We need to receive spiritual instruction from our pastor, youth leader, and Sunday school teacher. To put it in the words of the Bible: "Let us not give up meeting together, as some are in the habit of doing, but let us encourage one another—and all the more as you see the Day approaching."

To only attend the parties is like saying, "I'll take the dessert, but don't give me any meat." I encourage you to become regular and involved in your church and youth group. You'll be surprised at how much it will enhance your spiritual growth.

Q. Someday I'd like to read the entire Bible. Is that even possible?

A. Wow! I totally admire your desire to do that! Yes, it's possible. In fact, if you visit your local Christian bookstore, you'll see there are Bibles specifically put together so people can easily read them in one year. They're called "One-Year Bibles."

But you don't have to buy a new Bible to read the whole thing in a year. You can do what I'm doing. When

I was growing up, my dad told me if I read three sections every day and five sections on Sunday, I'd have the entire Bible read in one year. So that's what I'm doing. Only *this* year, I wanted to add a special twist to the challenge. I'm reading the Bible in a year . . . but I'm reading it through on my knees.

If you really want to read the Bible in a year, get a Bible you understand. Did you know there are Bibles published for girls your age? Check out Zondervan's *Young Women of Faith Bible.* You'll love it! It's filled with cool graphics and special helps that explain the tough-to-understand Scriptures, and all kinds of fun activities, too!

Q. How can I share my faith without scaring all my friends away?

A. I'm so glad your friends have *you* for a friend! You sound like someone who truly cares about where your friends will spend eternity. That's so cool!

I believe God will bless your desire to share your faith. The very best way to witness is by your life. Did you know your actions speak a lot louder than your words? It's true! Words are important, but unless our actions back them up, our words don't mean a thing.

For example, let's say Emily often invites Jessica to church. Emily *says* that God is the answer and that she has a genuine joy from serving Jesus. But if she comes to school every day sulking, and if she gets angry every time she can't be first, Jessica might think twice about going to church with her. In other words,

Emily *says* she's happy and that Christ has made a difference in her life, but Jessica can't see the difference.

Christians are called to be different from the world. Romans 12:1–2 tells us to be transformed—that means *changed* from the inside out.

Ask God to shine through your life so clearly that your friends will notice there's something different about you. And when you're having something special at church, invite them. If they ask you questions about why you're happy or different or so involved with your youth group, be ready to tell them. But the biggest influence on others will be with your lifestyle. If you have a strong, growing relationship with Jesus, others *will* notice!

Q. I love Jesus with all my heart, but since I read the book SHE SAID YES, I feel like I don't have as much of God as I should. I want to get closer to him, but I never do. Help!

A. One surefire way to get closer to God is the same way you get closer to a friend—spend time with him. The more you talk with him (prayer), and the more you read his personal letter to you (the Bible), the better you'll get to know him.

As you know, *She Said Yes* by Misty Bernall is the story of Cassie Bernall—the teen girl who was shot when a student holding a gun to her face asked if she believed in God. Cassie stood up for her beliefs, didn't she?

God may or may not ask you to die for him, but he *does* want you to be strong enough to stand up for him.

Where does that kind of strength come from? How can you get it?

It comes from Jesus Christ. And you get it by totally surrendering your life to him. A fully surrendered life is the life of someone who lets God be in total control.

Keep in mind that the Christian life is also a growth process. The more you walk with Jesus, the better you get to know him and understand his plan for your life. Trust him to provide you with all the strength you need exactly when you need it.

Q. *I'd like to start a Bible study with my friends. Any suggestions?*

A. I encourage you to begin with the gospel of John. It's a great book with all the basic information about Jesus—who he is, what his mission was, why he died, the difference he wants to make in our lives, and how he lives today.

You can take turns reading through one section at a time and discussing it. If you feel you need help, ask your Sunday school teacher, youth leader, or one of your parents to sit in with the group at first.

Q. Why do good people die when God can stop it?

A. Wow! You've asked a question that millions of people have been asking for years! In fact, entire books have been written on this subject.

We die because of sin in the world. Way back when God first created the world and the first people—Adam and Eve—it was a pure world without sin. But when Adam and Eve gave in to temptation from Satan, sin entered their lives and has been rampant in the world ever since.

We don't always understand God's ways, and we never will until we get to heaven and can ask him everything. But try to make this your goal: Accept God's ways without having to understand them.

You see, that's where faith comes in. I double-dare you to memorize this verse and ask God to use it to help you: "Now faith is being sure of what we hope for and certain of what we do not see" (Hebrews 11:1).

Q. I've been a Christian for two years, but I feel like my flame has gone out. I'm not on fire for God anymore. My faith isn't exciting like it used to be.

A. All Christians experience "dry seasons" spiritually. That's okay . . . as long as you do something about it. Even though you probably don't *feel* like it, read your Bible anyway. And though you may not *want* to, make it a point to pray daily.

Spending time with God needs to become a good habit. You probably don't always want to brush your teeth, but you do because you know it's right. It becomes a good habit. Brushing your teeth will always be boring, but spending time with God only gets better and better. The more you get into the habit of spending time with God, the more natural it will become.

Ask him to help and guide you through this dry time. And remember—it's just as important to remain close to Christ when you're numb and confused as it is when you're excited and on fire.

I triple-dog-dare you to memorize this Scripture: "Fight the good fight of the faith. Take hold of the eternal life to which you were called when you made your good confession in the presence of many witnesses" (1 Timothy 6:12).

Q. I am totally in love with God! But I'm discouraged. The other kids at my church don't care at all about their relationship with Christ. The only reason they even come to church is because their parents make them. I feel so alone in my faith!

A. I admire your spiritual depth and your desire to grow stronger in Christ. Have you spoken with your youth leader or pastor about this? He may have some ideas that will help.

Meanwhile, consider starting a Bible study, but don't call it that. Begin with munchies and a couple of games, then have a few lighthearted questions that everyone can go around the circle and take turns answering. I suggest having five questions for the first meeting. Create the last two questions to go deeper and to cause the kids to think more seriously about Christ.

Here's an example of a set of questions beginning lightly then gradually deepening:

1. *If you could star on any TV show, which one would it be and why?*
2. *What's the most memorable birthday or Christmas gift you've ever received?*
3. *If you had to compare your life to one of the following, which would it be and why? (a) a desert, (b) a mountain, (c) an ocean, (d) a cave*
4. *What do you need most in your life right now? (a) peace, (b) direction, (c) forgiveness, (d) meaning*
5. *What's keeping you from becoming all God wants you to be?*

Close in prayer and invite them to come back next week. After a few weeks, those who aren't interested will drop out, but the ones who are tuned in to going deeper will continue coming.

Q. *I feel God is calling me to be a missionary somewhere in Asia. The thing is ... I don't really want to be a missionary. Yeah, it's great to preach his good news of salvation, but I get scared thinking about all the persecution Christians experience in other countries. I feel lousy inside for thinking this way. What can I do?*

A. It's natural to be frightened when we hear about Christians in Sudan, Africa, and other parts of the world being killed for their faith. I suggest you read a book called *Jesus Freaks* by dc Talk. It's a wonderful account of dedicated Christians who gave their lives for their faith. It may help you understand the depth of their commitment.

No one looks forward to dying! And God knows that. He understands your fear. But guess what—he doesn't want you to be scared. He wants to replace that fear with a deep settled peace.

If God wants you to be a missionary, and you refuse, you'll be miserable. But think about this: If God calls you to be a missionary, he'll equip you and provide you with everything you need to do the job. He'll be your confidence. He'll give you the words to say. He'll be your strength.

I think the prophet Jeremiah was in his preteen years when he had this conversation with God:

> "Ah, Sovereign LORD," I said, "I do not know how to speak; I am only a child."
>
> But the LORD said to me, "Do not say, 'I am only a child.' You must go to everyone I send you to and say whatever I command you. Do not be afraid of them, for I am with you and will rescue you," declares the LORD.
>
> Then the LORD reached out his hand and touched my mouth and said to me, "Now, I have put my words in your mouth."
>
> (JEREMIAH 1:6–9)

And it could be that God simply wants your *willingness* to be a missionary. Once you're willing, he may change your direction. Why don't we pray about it, okay?

Dear Jesus,

I sense that you're calling me to be a missionary. I want to obey you, Father, but I'm really really scared! I don't wanna die. And I don't want to leave my family and friends.

But, Jesus, I want your will for my life—not my own will. You're in charge of me. I'll go wherever you send me, and I'll do whatever you ask. I trust you to provide everything I need.

I give you my fear, Jesus. Replace it with your strong, deep peace. Help me to feel your presence. I love you, Father, and I trust you with my future. Amen.

Q. I go to a Christian school, and I'm having some conflicts with my Bible teacher on the subject of baptism. Should I make an issue of it? Should I

say something in class to disagree with him? Or should I just keep quiet and let him talk?

A. There are several issues that Christians have varying opinion on. Baptism, speaking in tongues, and the Rapture are just a few of those issues.

You probably won't change his mind. And since he's employed by the school, it could be that he's been told by the administration to teach this specific view on baptism.

I encourage you to discuss your views with your parents, and if you *do* decide to share your beliefs with him, ask your parents to accompany you. Make it clear that you don't want your grade to be affected simply because you disagree with his theology.

Q. I have a friend who's not a Christian. One day we were talking about having a sleepover. I suggested she spend the night at my house on Saturday so she could go to church with my family and me. As soon as I mentioned church, she made a disgusted face and said, "Church?!" I want to witness to her, but I don't want to be forceful. Any ideas?

A. Continue to invite her. And whenever you *do* talk about church, tell her why you enjoy it so much. Since she made a face when you mentioned church, she must have a bad idea of what it's about.

But don't give up on her! When I was in the ninth grade, I invited a girl named Debbie to church all year. She never came. But by the time I went to college, she had moved into my dorm. This was a Christian college, so you can imagine my surprise when I saw her there!

When I asked her what she was doing on campus, she said, "Susie, you'll never know how badly I wanted to come to church with you. You were always so excited about your youth group and about all God was doing in your life. But my parents wouldn't let me go.

"A few years later, though, some neighbors moved next door to us, and they were Christians. They became friends with my parents and we all started going to church. We're Christians now, and I'm here at this Christian college so I can grow closer to God while I'm in school.

"I'm sorry I wasn't able to go to church with you back in the ninth grade, but I want you to know that you planted a seed."

Wow! I sure was excited. God would love to plant some spiritual seeds through you in the life of your friend. He may want someone else to come along and make that seed grow, but he can sure use you to get things started.

So again, don't give up. Keep inviting her to church—even if she never accepts. Keep loving her, and keep praying for her.

Q. How do I know what God wants me to do when I "grow up"?

A. Ask him. He'll let you know. But he may not tell you immediately. You see, God's timing is different than ours. He's never early . . . but he's also never late.

Guess what! There's a bigger issue here . . . and that is, "What does God want you to do right now?"

He doesn't want to wait until you're grown to use you to make a difference. He wants to use your life right now! That's why it's so important to have a strong, growing relationship with him right now.

How do you do that? By reading your Bible consistently and by talking with him. If you're not used to reading your Bible every day, start small. I suggest you read your Bible for one minute every single day. And pray for at least one minute every single day.

After you've done that for a few weeks, you'll probably be doing it for longer than one minute, and you won't even realize it. Getting to know Jesus is fun! And spending time with him is the greatest!

Questions About School

Q. There are a bunch of students at my school who make fun of me. It really hurts. What should I do?

A. I'd talk with your school counselor or teacher privately, and let them know how hurt you are. Do you have any idea why they're making fun of you? Is there anything you can do to make the situation better? For example, when they make fun of you, don't return insults with them. That only adds fuel to the fire.

Continue smiling. Keep being nice to everyone. Ask God to help you find one friend who won't make fun of you. And remember: Be the kind of friend to someone else that you'd like to have.

Q. I have a collection for Compassion International, but my English teacher doesn't believe there are really countries in need. "Those commercials are fake," he says. "They probably tell the kid he can't move from that mud puddle until they're finished filming. And they're probably dangling a sandwich in front of him."

I really respect my teacher, but now I'm confused. What's the truth?

A. It would be hard to believe there actually *aren't* countries in need unless we never looked at a newspaper or magazine and never listened to TV or radio news. The facts are simple: There are Third World countries (those in great need, high unemployment rates, and extreme poverty)—like Haiti. Developing countries (a step up from a Third World country in education, employment, and not as much poverty)—like Thailand. Developed or thriving countries (there is still poverty in some areas, but it's not rampant, the educational system is in place and the majority of citizens are educated, and the employment rate is good)—like the U.S., Canada, and most of Europe.

It's easier for me to believe your teacher is just giving you a hard time than to believe he really doesn't know about the great needs in Haiti, Cambodia, Kosovo, and other Third World areas.

There are several child-development organizations, and Compassion International is only one among many. But there are some major differences in Compassion that make it stand head and shoulders above others. You can tell your teacher that *U.S. News and World Report* ranked Compassion among the highest in all existing child-development organizations, because they actually use the money the way they say they will.

In other words, when you give money to a child, it really does help the child. How do I know? Because I've been on several overseas trips with Compassion, and I've been privileged to see firsthand how the money is used and the incredible difference it truly does make in a child's life.

For $32 a month, you can ensure that a child receives clothing, an education in a Christian school, tutoring, a hot meal each day, school supplies—and best of all, he'll learn about Jesus Christ.

Any organization that offers the above for much less than this price is not really putting the money where they say it's going. But why take my word for it? Call their toll-free number and ask them to send you information (1-800-336-7676). Show it to your teacher. Who knows? Maybe it'll change his mind and your class can end up sponsoring a child in Africa!

Q. *I'm home schooled, and my parents both work fulltime, and they don't discipline me at all with my schoolwork. Should I go back to public school? I'm always lonely.*

A. It must be really tough to be home alone and expected to work on your studies. I don't think I could have been disciplined enough to do that on my own, either.

Since neither of your parents are actually schooling you, I'd tell them how difficult it is for you to be so totally alone during the day. Maybe they don't realize you want and need one of them to be involved in your schoolwork with you. Most home schoolers are connected with other home schoolers in an association. But it sounds like you really are on your own.

Hopefully, once you've made your feelings known to your parents, they'll be able to make some changes that will allow them to be more involved in your home schooling or will enable you to return to public school.

Q. A girl who sits next to me in school always asks to look at someone's homework. Yesterday, she asked if she could see mine. I didn't think too much about it, but when I showed it to her she copied the answers. It makes me mad that she thinks she can just do this! It took me almost an hour to do all that homework.

Since she always asks to see someone's work, I'm afraid she'll want to *see mine again, and I don't want to give it to her. What do I do?*

A. I understand your not wanting to give your homework away, and I'm glad you're willing to take a stand against what she's doing. Cheating is always wrong—no matter what the circumstance!

If she asks to see your homework again, say something like this: "I put a lot of time and effort into getting my assignments finished. No way am I gonna just *give* this away. It's not fair, and it's not right. *But* if you need help with your homework, just ask me. I'll be glad to get together with you after school."

If you notice that she continues asking kids for homework answers, I encourage you to speak with your teacher about the problem.

Q. *I'm doing lousy in school, and my parents are going to ground me if I don't improve my grades. Got any study tips?*

A. A lot of students don't really know *how* to study, so let's start with the basics, okay? Doing homework is different from studying. Homework usually involves activity—writing answers, working out problems, creating a report, doing research on a certain topic, etc.

Studying involves going over a specific section of your textbook or your notes and learning it for an upcoming test. Let's start with your notes.

Are you taking good notes during class? Anything your teacher writes on the board is usually important. Copy it down. Are you really listening to class lectures? In other words, when your teacher goes over material from your textbook, she's "lecturing." So pay special attention to what she's highlighting from your book. She wouldn't take the time to go over it verbally if it wasn't important. Make sure you make note of that.

When you're going over those notes and rereading your textbook material, do it in an area where you won't be disturbed. Trying to study at a skating rink is going to be a lot harder than in the library.

If you can find a place in your house where you can be totally alone, go there. No music. Good lighting. No TV. Just you and your study material. Before you actually begin studying, ask God to help you remember what you go over. After you feel you know the material pretty well, ask your mom or dad to quiz you on it.

Q. I've been home schooled for five years and am thinking about switching to public school. How do I know if it's God's will?

A. Let's talk about the advantages of each, okay? When you're home schooled, you can often work at a faster or slower pace than you can in public school. You don't have to face peer pressure or be exposed to things that could damage your faith. And the best part of being home schooled is that you can be taught by your parents who have a wonderful opportunity to instill *their* values in you instead of your being saturated with the world's views.

Some of the advantages of public school would be that students often have more opportunities to be involved in team sports and a variety of clubs. You have a lot more interaction with other students your age, and you get the chance to be a witness for Christ to those in your class who aren't Christians.

Switching from home school to public school is a big decision. One of the best ways you can know what to do is by allowing God to speak through your parents. What do *they* think? Have you talked with them about it? Ultimately, they're the ones who will make the decision. Sit down and talk through the advantages of both options and spend time praying about it as a family.

A Little Bit of Everything

Q. I'm the very last chair in my band section. How do I get the discipline to practice more?

A. I understand exactly how you feel. I used to play the violin, and I was never in first chair. Even though I wanted to move up, I guess I didn't want it badly enough to practice more.

If you really want to increase your practice time, ask your mom or dad to hold you accountable. Create a chart that will allow you to fill in and account for the amount of time you rehearse each day. It always helps to actually see on paper what's been done. You'll feel better about yourself as you gradually increase your practice time. But that's the key—do it gradually. Start by increasing your time for five minutes each day for a week. Then increase it to 10 minutes each day. You'll be moving up in your band section before you know it!

Q. I baby-sit and have saved enough money to buy some things that I really want, like CDs and some cool sunglasses. But my parents keep telling me to save my money. What good is having money if I can't spend it?

A. The cool thing about saving is that your money adds up a lot faster than you think. And it's also good to get into the habit of not spending your money every time you see something you want.

Ask your parents if they'll consider a compromise. For instance, would they be willing to settle for you saving 10 percent, tithing 10 percent, and spending the rest? It's certainly worth a discussion.

Q. I want to be an actress really really bad! Of course, I'll use my talent for God. How do I get into acting?

A. Check the yellow pages for agents. Ask your mom to make an appointment for you to visit an agent so you can find out how to break into the biz.

But unless you live in or near a major city such as Los Angeles, New York, or Washington D.C., it can be tough. I suggest you use your talent right where you are to begin with. Act in your school play, try out for your local city theater. Start a skit group or drama team at church.

Q. I've always wanted to help people. But what can someone who's only ten years old do?

A. You can do a lot! One person can make a huge difference! Did you know one vote saved President Andrew Johnson from getting impeached in 1868? And way back in 1776, one vote determined that the official language of America would be English instead of German. And Adolph Hitler was made head of the Nazi Party by just one vote in 1923.

Never underestimate the power of one. And when that *one* is filled with Jesus Christ and energized by him, there's no limit on what he'll do through your life!

I know of a young boy who had a heart for the homeless, so he started collecting blankets for them. He made national news.

Another youngster decided that children in foster care should have a quality suitcase with a stuffed animal inside. She got luggage companies and a toy company to support her and ended up being on *The Oprah Winfrey Show* because of the positive difference she made.

You can write encouraging letters to your congressmen. You can write letters to TV station managers when you disagree with television programming. You can make your mom's day by cleaning the entire house for her without being asked. You can help change a friend's life for eternity by praying with her and leading her to Christ.

Tell God that you want to be a positive influence on those around you, and ask him to give you opportunities to make a difference, and he will.

Q. I know it's wrong to gossip, but what can I say to politely stop it? How do I answer someone — especially an adult — who says, "What do you think of Samantha?" or "Do you know anything about Tim and Jessica?"

A. When you're talking about someone who's not around, it's not always gossip. For example, "Tim mows lawns" isn't really gossip. It's simply a fact. Also, when you become concerned about harmful behavior you see in your friends, it is appropriate to tell a trustworthy adult. But a remark meant to hurt or belittle someone is gossip—and it's always wrong.

Why not try some positive gossip? It's really fun to spread good news about people. I love telling others that Marty McCormack, our associate editor for *Brio* magazine, is in complete charge of our Web site. (Check it out at www.briomag.com.) I love saying, "Have you seen what Marty's been up to? Get to a computer!"

When you hear negative gossip, try to turn it around to positive gossip. Or say, "I'm really trying to only say positive stuff about people. Please excuse me." Then walk away.

Q. My parents are making me take piano lessons. I hate it! What good is it?

A. Hey, I know where you're coming from! I used to have to take piano, too. I enjoyed being able to play when I could choose what I wanted to play. But other than that, I didn't really enjoy it.

Even though you're not having fun right now, try to realize what you're learning is valuable. Having a basic background in music can help in a lot of areas. For instance, it'll help you learn the songs faster when you're singing in church. And when you're 20, you may decide you'd like to be part of a cool band in college.

It also helps you gain some discipline. Ask your parents what kind of timeline they're thinking about. Are they wanting you to take lessons forever, or just for two years? It will seem a lot easier if you can see an end in sight and know how long your piano playing is going to last.

Q. My class at school is going to start track during PE. I've always been a good runner, and I'm scared I might run faster than the boys. Will this mean they won't like me?

A. Some of them might not. But if they don't, they're the kind of guys who wouldn't make good friends anyway. A real friend likes you just the way you are—even if you're better at some things than he is.

My advice? Do your best. Run your fastest, and don't worry what anyone else is going to think. Give it all you've got!

Q. I'm twelve years old and very imaginative and dramatic. When I was younger, I loved to play "dress up" and "dolls." So what's the problem? Well . . . I still like to do these things.

The other day a younger girl was at our house, and we dressed up and played outside. Then when I realized our fourteen-year-old neighbor girl was looking for me, I ran inside and hid. I didn't want her to see me playing "dress up."

I've talked with my mom about it, and she tells me I'm normal. But I've never seen any dolls or dress-up clothes in my friends' rooms. I don't want to be weird. Should I give up these activities?

A. People mature at different rates. Some twelve-year-olds are thinking about boys and makeup, and other twelve-year-olds are happy playing hide-and-seek and riding bicycles.

Your friends may not admit it, but they probably still enjoy some of the same things you still do. It's totally okay (and yes, I agree with your mom: You're normal!) to still like playing "dress up" and "dolls."

When you want to be with your fourteen-year-old neighbor friend, do things she's interested in—like watching a video or taking a walk, etc. And when you're with your younger friends, feel free to play with dolls. In time, you'll get tired of "dressing up" and playing with dolls. But for now, enjoy it!

Q. Is it okay to listen to non-Christian music?

A. Depends on the lyrics. By non-Christian music, I'm assuming you don't mean the ballet or opera. (That can be non-Christian music, too.) You're probably talking about secular rock, alternative, or pop music.

If the lyrics promote actions that go against God's will, don't bother listening to it. For example, some bands sing about sex and killing, and are full of anger.

There are also lots of secular songs full of positive things such as peace, love, and joy. This is a great topic to discuss with your parents. They can help you make wise music choices based on the songs' lyrics.

Q. My parents and friends think I'm weird because I love all animals and think they're beautiful—even snakes, sharks, and crocodiles. I just don't know how to prove to them that any animal in the world is precious and wonderful. Any suggestions? I feel very different from everyone else.

A. While every animal is God's creation, I have to admit I don't think all of them are "precious" as you say. I'm scared of snakes, and I sure wouldn't want to run into an angry rhino anytime soon!

Maybe God has given you a special love for animals for a reason. He may call you into a special kind of veterinarian missions endeavor. Or maybe he just wants to use you in a wonderful way with animals.

You'll probably never be able to "prove" to people that every single animal is "precious." They may never see all animals that way. But that's okay. You don't have to prove anything. Just continue to care for the animals God puts in your path.

As for feeling different from everyone else—take that as a special calling on your life. God dreams BIG dreams for you! Memorize Ephesians 3:20 for proof, okay?

Now to him who is able to do immeasurably more than all we ask or imagine, according to his power that is at work within us, to him be glory in the church and in Christ Jesus throughout all generations, for ever and ever!

Q. There's an eleven-year-old girl at my school who keeps threatening me and my friends. Talking it out won't work like teachers tell you. This is serious! She has tried to hurt me. Can you give me some advice that'll work?

I tried ignoring her, but that doesn't help. We walk the same way home, and I'm scared she'll beat me up—she would really do that! One time she beat up a girl right in front of the principal. She's nothing but trouble.

A. There's a reason this girl is being so mean, and I'm guessing it's because she's hurting inside. This may be the only way she can get attention. Your parents need to talk with the principal and explain how frightened you are.

Q. How do I talk to people and get a conversation going?

A. Asking questions is a great way to start a conversation. Since people usually enjoy talking about themselves, ask questions that will help you get to know the person better. And try not to ask questions that require only a yes or no answer. Ask questions that will get the person talking. Here are some examples:

- *"What grade are you in, and what's your favorite subject?" (If you enjoy that subject also, comment on it.)*
- *"What do you like to do for fun?" (Next, share what you enjoy doing—playing basketball, go-carting, rollerblading, etc.)*
- *"If you could invite anyone in the world to your next birthday party, who would it be and why?"*

Another great tip is to try to find some common ground. Are you the same age? Do you both go to church? Did you each take a vacation last summer? The more you have in common, the easier it will be to keep a conversation going.

Q. I'd love to be a model. It seems like a fun and easy way to make money. Any suggestions?

A. Professional models will tell you it's not easy to be photographed eight hours a day under bright lights and in heavy makeup. Check your yellow pages for modeling agencies, but beware that many of them try to "sell" young girls on modeling by taking financial advantage of them.

I have a couple of friends who are professional models in New York. They're Christians, and they want to help young girls make wise choices when it comes to modeling. For more information, check out their Web site at www.modelsforchrist.com.

Q. My parents let me have a party with guys and girls, but they told me kissing was not allowed under any circumstances. Well, my friends wanted to play spin-the-bottle—you know—where everyone sits in a circle and you spin a bottle. Whomever it points to selects someone to kiss.

I explained to everyone that my parents wouldn't allow it, but my friends kept trying to talk me into it, saying stuff like, "Your folks won't know because they're upstairs."

I still didn't allow the game to be played, and I know I did the right thing. But I feel like a party pooper. My friends are making me feel like a big loser. This party just didn't turn out like I thought it would.

A. Hey, I'm really really really proud of you for not giving in! This proves to your parents that you can be trusted to do what's right—even when they're not looking and the pressure is on. You go, Girl!

The key to not letting something happen that you don't want to happen is to have a plan. Wa-a-a-ay before the party starts (like a couple of weeks ahead of time), figure out what the entire evening will look like in terms of games, videos, music, munchies, outdoor activities, and how much time will be spent on each event.

When there's spare time available, people get bored. And when they get bored, they tend to come up with unwise choices.

Q. *I know lying and cheating is wrong. But what about going to parties?*

A. It depends on the party. Are you trying to sneak off to a party behind your parents' backs? Hey, that's never right! And you'll always regret it.

What's going to be happening at the party? If you don't know, let that be a warning sign. Is there going to be alcohol? Are you going to be pressured into playing some kind of kissing game? Will anyone try to sneak in cigarettes or drugs?

Find out everything ahead of time, and get your parents' permission. If they say no, obey them . . . but consider having your own party! Ask your parents to help you plan the biggest bash you can think of. Make a list of what kind of food and drinks you want to serve (Kool-Aid, Coca-Cola, orange drink, tea, or burgers, sandwiches, pizza, hot dogs), and then make a list of everyone you want to invite. Assign everyone to bring something off your food and beverage list—so you don't have to get everything.

Then ask some friends to help you plan some games. If it's an all-girl party, you could have a great time doing makeovers on each other or making some cool crafts. If it's a guy/girl party, you may want to have some outdoor stuff planned such as backyard volleyball, croquet, or trampoline fun.

Q. Is it wrong to dream about marriage and having kids and kissing your husband?

A. God created women with a "mothering instinct," so it's natural to dream about having a husband and a family. He also made us sexual beings, so it's normal to wonder what it will be like to kiss your husband.

But let me encourage you to talk to God while you're dreaming about these things. Talk to him about the qualities you think are important in a husband. Ask him to provide the right man for you someday. Pray for your children. (That seems funny, doesn't it? But you can actually begin praying for them *now* wa-a-a-ay before you're married and give birth!) Remember, God already knows who your children are—even before they're born.

Wanna pray right now?

Dear Jesus:
Someday, I want to be married to a wonderful man who loves me and takes great

care of me. I also want to have children who will grow up to glorify you.

Jesus, it feels romantic to think about kissing my future husband and being held by him.

Please help me not to get so carried away with the romance of it all that I forget to let you be in charge of finding the right man. Help me never to get into a dating relationship just to date someone. And help me never to kiss a boy just to kiss him. I realize my kisses are extremely valuable. So help me be incredibly choosy about whom I kiss. In fact, you help me with those decisions, okay?

I love you, Father. And I thank you for my future husband and children. Help my future husband to come to know you at an early age. Strengthen him today, Jesus. Help him to become a godly man. Amen.

Q. A lot of my friends have a collection. I want one, too, but I can't think of anything to collect.

A. Collecting something special can be a ton of fun! I collect Coca-Cola bottles and cans from around the world. But there's a catch—the can or bottle has to be full of Coke—unopened! I especially like the ones that have Coca-Cola written in a foreign language on them.

The key to having a fun collection is to decide on something that's not impossible to get but is still a challenge. If it's too easy, you'll lose interest. And it also needs to be something you can afford. I have a friend who collects Precious Moments figurines, but since they're so expensive, I decided on Cokes. (Hey, when I fly internationally, I can get them free from the flight attendant!)

I'll give you some other ideas, and you complete the list with some of your own, okay?

- *postcards*
- *coins*
- *matchbooks*
- *pencils with funny tops on them*
- *stamps*
-
-
-
-

Q. I want to have a baby so bad. I'm only 11, but I really think I'm ready to take care of a baby.

A. I'm guessing you're wanting a baby because you want something or someone to love and to love you back. Babies don't know how to love. They're cute, and they're cuddly, but they're also sick and messy and in tears a lot.

It's not God's will that you have a baby outside of marriage, and since you're only 11, you've got a few years to wait. But *never* get married just so you can have a baby! That's not a good reason to spend your life with someone. Determine to only marry a godly man you love and who loves you back; someone who's committed to Jesus Christ and who brings out the very best in you.

Meanwhile, there *are* some ways you can get involved with babies. Ask your mom if you can volunteer to help out in your church nursery. I know our church nursery is always looking for helpers!

Also consider volunteering at your local humane society (the dog pound). Okay, so a dog isn't a child . . . it will still give you a chance to provide care and to be of service. I think you'll enjoy it!

Q. I'm twelve years old, and I love to write poetry and stories. I'd like to get some of my writing published. How do I make this happen?

A. I suggest you take a peek at *The Writer's Market.* It's an annual book, so a new one comes out every

January. It contains publishers from around the nation—book publishers, greeting card publishers, video publishers, magazine publishers, etc.—and will tell you which ones accept freelance material. (That means an editor didn't call and ask you to write something; you just wrote it and want to send it in.)

You'd be surprised at how many preteens and teenagers get published. I used to teach a high school creative writing class and at the beginning of each year I'd explain *The Writer's Market* and how to use it. I challenged my students to get published sometime during the year. The cool part was if anyone got published, I promised him an automatic A for the entire semester. Guess what—three kids got published!

And maybe you can, too! You can find *The Writer's Market* in the reference section of your local library, or you can buy it from any secular bookstore. Good luck!

Q. I want to baby-sit to earn money, but no one ever asks me. What can I do to make my services known?

A. If you have a computer, you can print some brochures. If you don't, you can still make some posters. Give your services a name (like "Julianne's Baby-sitting Services"), and provide enough information about yourself that will help parents feel you're trustworthy.

Include your name, phone number, and address. Also provide some references (nice things other adults have said about you, such as "Julianne baby-sat my three-year-old daughter and did a wonderful job."—Mrs. Walker).

The number of flyers you can make will determine how many you can distribute. If you have enough, you could put them under windshield wipers on cars in a crowded parking lot, or pass them out door-to-door and meet your neighbors.

You may also want to consider getting some business cards made. This might cost a little money, but it could be worth the effort!

Q. What's the deal with power bracelets? Is it okay to wear them?

A. Power bracelets have their roots in Buddhism. Many Buddhists believe they receive special power from the bracelets. Of course, only Jesus gives real and lasting power. If we think beads or a statue or a certain pair of shoes can give us power, we're looking at that item as an idol.

God warns us several times throughout the Bible not to let idols into our lives. In other words, he wants us to know—beyond all doubt—that he is the One who empowers us, saves us, and guides us. In return, we should want to serve him with loving devotion and commitment.

Is it wrong to wear the beads? I don't think a bead in itself is a sin. We have to go a little deeper. Why do you want to wear them? Do you simply want some red beads to go with your red dress? Fine. Are you wanting these particular beads because everyone else has them and you think they'll help you become more popular? Wrong.

Talk with your parents about them and pray about it. God will either give you a peace about it or an uneasy feeling. Follow his lead.

Q. I've grown a lot closer to God this year, and I want to serve him in a special way. The youth group at my church is going on a missions trip to Mexico, and even though I'm only twelve, we're considered a part of the youth group.

I really want to go! So what's the problem? My parents are afraid I won't be safe. They're scared that anything could happen. How can I convince them to let me go?

A. Ask your youth pastor if he has a video or anything your parents can look at that will give them more information about where you'll be and what you'll be doing. Face it—anything can happen overseas! International travel can be downright frightening at times.

I travel quite a bit, and have been to every continent in the world except Antarctica. God has protected me, but I think he also expects me to use common sense. For instance, I wouldn't travel to a country that's known for danger or is politically unstable. So the more information your parents can get on this trip, the better!

Also, ask your folks if they'll consider being sponsors. This way, you'd still get to participate in the trip, and they'd get to see firsthand what's involved.

If they still don't have a peace about it and won't let you go, respect their decision. After all, missions is something in which you need God's blessing *and* your parents' blessing. It could be the timing just isn't right. Who knows? In two years, your parents may feel totally different. Be willing to show your maturity during the next few years and continue to pray about it. God can certainly change your parents' hearts if he eventually wants you on a missions trip.

Meanwhile, be a missionary right where you are! Visit a nursing home. Offer to rake someone's yard. Take some lemonade to someone who's sick. You don't have to go overseas to make a difference! God can use you right now—right here.

Q. *All the guys in my class pick on me for laughing too much. I can't help it! Things are just really funny to me. I'm afraid if I keep laughing, I'll become a freak and everyone will pick on me. How do I stop?*

A. Sounds to me like these guys aren't really picking on you—they're teasing you. I think they actually like your giggle and are giving you a "hard time" because they enjoy being around you.

If you were hauling out a fake laugh, people would know. And that would *really* be obnoxious! (Ask your mom to be honest with you and tell you if your laugh is offensive.) But there's nothing more refreshing than being around someone who sees the humor in things and can lighten up the situation with some laughter.

I think you have a special gift, and I'm excited that you see so much humor around you. Keep it up!

Q. I'm nine years old, and I'm an MK (missionary kid) living in the Philippines. We just got here four months ago. I miss my friends in America. And I miss all the everyday conveniences such as big grocery stores and malls and TV shows I can understand. Will I ever feel like this is home?

A. I think you'll eventually feel at home in the Philippines, but it may take a while. Your family has made a huge change, and changes are never easy. It takes a while to adjust.

Think of this move as an adventure! You'll get to experience stuff most kids can only dream about. There are so many advantages to being a missionary kid. Check out what a few MK friends of mine say about their lives and where they live:

> *"Living overseas has made me much more dependent on God."*
>
> —RUTH ENOS, GAMBIA, WEST AFRICA

"I've been able to find my identity in the Lord Jesus Christ. In His Kingdom, one's nationality doesn't matter. I've found that the kind of life you have—whether good or bad—is not based as much on surroundings as on the attitude the person has toward that which surrounds him."

—STEPHEN MCKINNEY, MADRID, SPAIN

"God is teaching us that He is everything we need, and though we sometimes don't feel accepted in this world, we're totally accepted in His world. As a result, He's becoming our Lord, Master, Comforter, best Friend, Shepherd ... everything!"

—BRIA AND LINDSAY BLESSING, LVIV, UKRAINE

"The best advantage of being an MK is learning different cultures and languages. I think it's pretty cool that my family is out here. We're not here just to say we've been to Africa or that we can speak another language. We're here for the most important reason of all—to tell the Africans about Jesus Christ."

—AUTUMN JOY MORGAN, CÔTE D'IVOIRE, WEST AFRICA

"Bagabag is one of the most fun places in the Philippines to be! My friends and I build forts in the gullies, play tennis, and go swimming a lot because it's so hot here."

—MAY MCCLELLAND, NUEVA VIZCAYO, PHILIPPINES

"Watching people receive God's holy Word in their own native tongue is really cool. It gets especially exciting when I see someone hearing the gospel for the very first time. Wow!"

—CORRIE MANTELL, SURINAME, SOUTH AMERICA

I spoke at Faith Academy—a Christian school in Manila, Philippines—a few years ago and was so impressed with the students. I think MKs are some of the sharpest kids around! Give it time. I think you'll eventually grow to love where you are.

Meanwhile . . . ask God to give you a special ministry in the Philippines. This will help you realize you're not there simply because of your parents' ministry, but that God wants to use *you* as well!

Q. Four months ago, I fell head over heels in love with a celebrity. My mind is focused on him 24/7 (24 hours a day, seven days a week)! I'm getting bad grades because I can't concentrate, and I'm driving myself crazy.

He's seven years older than me, but I'll die if he marries someone else! I've prayed for help, and I've tried doing things to keep my mind off of him, but I still think about him constantly. What else can I do?

A. It's hard to fall in love with someone we don't really know. Can I suggest that you're *infatuated* with him instead? And you're infatuated with what you see on the screen—a perfectly made-up guy with no zits, perfect hair, fresh breath, great personality.

But if you could really observe him 24/7, you'd notice that he may get angry for no reason at all, he may be impatient, he wakes up with a bed-head and bad breath, and he may even be rude.

Though no one is perfect, celebrities are positioned to *appear* perfect. What would happen if you began to think about Jesus Christ as much as you think about this guy?

Wow! Your life would probably take a 180-degree turn! Who knows the incredibly exciting things God would do with your life if you'd be radically sold-out to him?

Wanna try it? Let's pray.

Dear Jesus:

I admit, I'm totally obsessed with this guy. I think about him all the time, and I fantasize about him loving me. I'm beginning to realize that you don't want me to focus all my attention on him. You want my attention. You want my mind. You want my love and my devotion.

So, Jesus, will you forgive me for going so crazy over this guy? I don't wanna be

obsessed with him anymore. I want to be saturated with you.

Take control of my thought life, Father.
And help me to think about pure things.

I love you, Jesus. Amen.

Want some help in getting your thoughts off of him?
Try memorizing a new Scripture verse each week.
Here's one to start with: "Finally, brothers, whatever
is true, whatever is noble, whatever is right, whatever
is pure, whatever is lovely, whatever is admirable—if
anything is excellent or praiseworthy—think about
such things" (Philippians 4:8).

Q. I recently quit listening to secular music and
am wanting to begin listening to Christian music.
But where do I start? There are so many
groups, I don't know where to begin.

A. Most Christian bookstores have listening stations.
This enables the customer to sit down, put headphones
on, and listen to a variety of CDs without having to buy
any. This is a fantastic way to find out if you like a group
before spending money on them. Also consider checking
out musicforce.com and other similar sites on the Web.

There are so-o-o-o many great Christian bands
today, it can be tough to know where to begin, though.

So what kind of music do you like? Pop? Rock? Alternative? Country? Tell one of the clerks what kind of music you're interested in, and he can help you find some Christian music with that sound. Then head over to the listening station, put on the headphones, and start jamming!

Q. *I'm confused about all my feelings. All my friends say I'm normal, but I begin almost every day feeling depressed. I feel pulled in so many directions. Help!*

A. What *is* depression? Sara says, "I bombed the science test. I'm so depressed!" Is she really depressed? Or is she just totally bummed?

Ericka says, "I can't believe I didn't make the team! I'm totally depressed." She's not actually in a state of depression. She'll try out again next year. Meanwhile, she'll find other activities to participate in.

Depression is a deep state of hopelessness. Sometimes it's caused by circumstances and other times it's caused by a chemical imbalance in the brain. Often it can be helped with medication prescribed by a doctor.

Please know that it's *normal* for you to be confused during your preteen and teen years. It really is! Everything inside (and even on the outside) of your body is changing! Not only that, but you're at the point where you'll soon begin changing classes at school. It can feel like your entire world is turning upside down.

You say you begin each day feeling depressed. If you're not really in such a state of depression that you can't put one foot in front of the other or make yourself get up and get dressed, can't you say instead that you begin each day feeling down?

You may dread going to school. Maybe you're not ready to give that oral report that's due today. And perhaps you're hoping you won't run into Jeremy. That stuff gets you down. But you're probably not depressed. (If you still think you *are* depressed, talk to your parents about visiting your family doctor.)

Let's try this: Begin each day by talking to Jesus. Know what I did during junior high? I'd walk over to my bedroom window, open the curtains, look up at the sky, and say, "I believe in Susie Shellenberger. I am a star of the universe. Lord, teach me that you love me today."

That did several things for me. It helped me strengthen my self-esteem. It reminded me that in God's eyes, I'm incredible—no matter what anyone else thinks. And it also taught me to actively look for ways that God was going to show his love to me that day.

Will you try it? I think you'll be surprised at the difference God can make through a simple, heartfelt prayer.

Q. I saw a man on the corner with a sign that said "Will work for food." It broke my heart. I've spent so much money on pizza and concert tickets and CDs. How can I help?

A. Wow! What a tender heart you have! And guess what—God can certainly do a lot with a heart like yours! Many people don't give money to the homeless, because they assume the homeless will spend that money on drugs or alcohol. And maybe some do. But I believe there are some genuinely hungry folks who really would use that money for a meal.

Consider talking with your pastor about making a special deal with a local restaurant. Would the restaurant be willing to sell your church some "coupons" at a discounted price good for one meal? The understanding would be that *you* wouldn't use them to eat at the restaurant, but that people in your church would buy them and keep them handy in their car so that when they see someone begging for food, they can give him a special coupon good for a meal at this specific restaurant.

Most cities have a soup kitchen that feeds the homeless. I have a friend who serves in the Colorado Springs Soup Kitchen once a month. She really enjoys it, and it gives her an opportunity to be a blessing to others.

I know a high school girl in the Kansas City area who volunteers every Tuesday evening to tutor the homeless. There are several ways you, too, can help. Ask your parents and your pastor to help you discover the areas of need in your hometown.

Q. I think it would be so fun to have a pen pal, but I don't know how to get one. Do you know of any pen pal clubs?

A. Yes! *Clubhouse* magazine (for ages 8 to 12) and *Brio* magazine for teen girls (ages 12 and up) both offer pen pal clubs. These magazines are published by Focus on the Family, and you can call their toll-free number for more information: 1-800-232-6459.

Q. My friend and I want to sing alternative music. We're both Christians and want to be famous for being modest. How can we get started? And is it bad for us to want to sing this type of music?

A. Is it bad to want to sing this music? Depends. Is it Christian alternative music? If so, I'm not concerned. If it's secular alternative music, you need to sit down and take a hard look at the lyrics.

I admire your desire to become known for modesty! So with that in mind, try to find songs with lyrics that reflect your beliefs. If you're dressing modestly but singing trashy alternative music, what good is that?

It's natural to want to be famous. Everyone desires to be known for something. But popularity isn't the most important thing in the world—your relationship with Christ is. What if it's not God's will that you be famous? Are you okay with that? Are you so in love with Jesus that you'll accept his plan for your life instead of being stuck on your own?

Why don't we talk to God about it right now?

Dear Father,

You know my desire to sing. Please help me to find the right music with lyrics that will bring glory to you. I admit, I'd love to be famous. But if that's not what you have in mind for me, I give that dream to you. I'd much rather have your plan for my life than my own dreams.

I love you, Father. Keep me close to you and guide me in the area of music. Amen.

Guess what! No matter how big your dreams are, God dreams bigger. I dare you to memorize the proof:

"For I know the plans I have for you," declares the LORD, "plans to prosper you and not to harm you, plans to give you hope and a future."

(*JEREMIAH 29:11*)

"For my thoughts are not your thoughts, neither are your ways my ways," declares the LORD.

(*ISAIAH 55:8*)

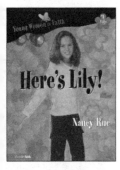

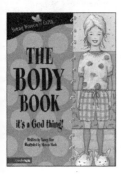

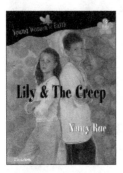
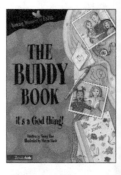

NIV Young Women of Faith Bible
GENERAL EDITOR SUSIE SHELLENBERGER

Designed just for girls ages 8-12, the *NIV Young Women of Faith Bible* not only has a trendy, cool look, it's packed with fun to read in-text features that spark interest, provide insight, highlight key foundational portions of Scripture, and more. Discover how to apply God's word to your everyday life with the *NIV Young Women of Faith Bible.*

Hardcover 0-310-91394-2

Zonder**kidz**™